STARITSA

STARITSA

THE SPIRITUAL MOTHERHOOD
OF CATHERINE DOHERTY

Donald A. Guglielmi

With a Foreword by Robert Wild

PICKWICK *Publications* · Eugene, Oregon

STARITSA
The Spiritual Motherhood of Catherine Doherty

Pickwick Publications
An Imprint of Wipf and Stock Publishers
199 W. 8th Ave., Suite 3
Eugene, OR 97401

www.wipfandstock.com

PAPERBACK ISBN: 978-1-4982-8940-5
HARDCOVER ISBN: 978-1-4982-8942-9
EBOOK ISBN: 978-1-4982-8941-2

Cataloguing-in-Publication data:

Names: Guglielmi, Donald. | Wild, Robert, foreword writer

Title: Staritsa : the spiritual motherhood of Catherine Doherty / Donald Guglielmi, with a foreword by Robert Wild.

Description: Eugene, OR: Pickwick Publications, 2018 | Includes bibliographical references.

Identifiers: ISBN 978-1-4982-8940-5 (paperback) | ISBN 978-1-4982-8942-9 (hardcover) | ISBN 978-1-4982-8941-2 (ebook)

Subjects: LCSH: Doherty, Catherine de Hueck, 1896–1985. | Christian life—Catholic authors | Spiritual direction—Catholic Church | Spiritual life—Christianity

Classification: BX4705.D56 G35 2018 (paperback) | BX4705.D56 (ebook)

Manufactured in the U.S.A.   11/28/17

Contents

Permissions

Cover photo reprinted with permission from Madonna House Apostolate, 2888 Dafoe Road, Combermere, Ontario KoJ 1Lo

All unpublished material from the Madonna House archives is printed with permission from Madonna House Apostolate, 2888 Dafoe Road, Combermere, Ontario KoJ 1Lo

Spiritual Direction in the Early Christian East.
Copyright 1990 by Cistercian Publications, Inc. © 2008 by Order of St. Benedict, Collegeville, Minnesota. Used with permission.

The Sayings of the Desert Fathers
Copyright 1975 by Benedicta Ward, SLG, trans. A Cistercian Series title published by Liturgical Press, Collegeville, Minnesota. Used with permission.

Unpublished material from General Archives of the Basilian Fathers used with permission.

Unpublished material from the American Catholic History Research Center used with permission.

Foreword

As the Servant of God Catherine Doherty becomes better known, more people are writing about her and researching her life and spirituality. Besides the publications of the community and articles in newspapers and magazines, some academic studies have been done. A significant milestone in what I call "Catherine Studies" was reached in 2003. I have the privilege and joy of introducing it here.

Madonna House has associate bishops, priests, and deacons, and one of our associate priests, Fr. Donald A. Guglielmi (of the Bridgeport, Connecticut diocese), successfully defended his thesis and became a Doctor of Sacred Theology. The topic of his thesis? *Staritsa: The Spiritual Motherhood of Catherine de Hueck Doherty*, from which the main sections for this present book have been taken. Here are some excerpts from Fr. Guglielmi's enthusiastic letter to me on that occasion:

> Yes, praise God, it is over and a total success. My second reader is a well-known professor of spiritual theology here in Rome, Fr. Paul Murray, OP. His personal view is important because of his stature in the Roman academic world as a spiritual theologian. When he read the thesis the second time he said, "*It burns you, like a flame. Catherine Doherty's spirituality shines forth and is a flame. I think she is a saint. The holiness of this woman is apparent in this work, and I think she stands a good chance of being beatified.*" Isn't that an interesting use of words, just like Catherine!
>
> He told me that this work must be published, "for the good of the Church." He asked me to seriously consider doing so. So our beloved Catherine has now been introduced to the heart of the Church at one of the oldest pontifical universities in the world— the Angelicum—where John Paul II received his doctorate. In fact, I defended my thesis today in the very same room where he did so in 1948.

In Fr. Guglielmi's letter he told me how he came to decide to write about Catherine:

> In April of 1997, I was at a point in my studies when I needed to choose a topic for my licentiate thesis that could later be expanded into a doctoral dissertation. At first I thought about St. Catherine of Genoa or Walter Hilton, but these would have involved archival work in Genoa or Britain, and seemed too burdensome. After two or three weeks without success, I began to panic as the deadline for choosing a topic approached.
>
> Then one night at the Casa Santa Maria dell'Umilta, where I resided, I had a very vivid dream that changed my life. In the dream I was standing before a larger than life size outline with four chapters. I "knew" (i.e., I was receiving this knowledge from a source outside myself) that the outline was about Catherine Doherty, the Little Mandate, and Madonna House. All this was clear, but I did not know what the outline was, or why I was there looking at it. I walked back and forth, puzzled, and examined it.
>
> Then I noticed that a woman was sitting directly behind the outline. I poked my head around and there was Catherine herself! She was dressed in a lovely pattern that fell below her knees. Her hair was tied back in a bun, and her face was radiant and full of joy and love. I asked her, "Excuse me, what is this?" She stood up, smiled and pointed her finger towards me, and said with a thick Russian accent, "Yes, Father, this is your dissertation. It is going to be easy and quite doable." I looked at her with amazement, and then woke from my dream.

Fr. Guglielmi's spiritual director agreed that this sounded like a genuine dream from God and that he should act on it. I think the inclusion of this account by Fr. Guglielmi in this Preface is very significant in relation to the theme of this book—Catherine's spiritual maternity. Just as she would give "words of life" to her spiritual children, she gave a "word" to Fr. Guglielmi through a dream.

Throughout the ages of faith, a certain kind of theology has been called "imaginative": "The hallmark of imaginative theology is that it 'thinks with' images, rather than propositions or scriptural texts or rarified inner experiences—although none of these are excluded. The devices of literature—metaphor, symbolism, allegory, dialogue, and narrative are its working tools."[1] I believe Catherine's theology was of this "imaginative" type. It will

1. Newman, *God and the Goddesses*, 298.

help if you keep this definition in mind as you read about Catherine's way of speaking of God and the things of God as Fr. Guglielmi presents it.

As mentioned above, when his dissertation was approved, Fr. Guglielmi's readers suggested that it should be published. However, they also recommended that it be considerably shortened. Some sections in the original, for example, were included simply to provide a broader picture to his theological readers and those unfamiliar with Catherine. These sections are not really necessary for audiences already familiar with Catherine's life and writings.

However, three sections that have been dropped from the original thesis for this edition are as follows: her biography, the Russian roots of her spirituality, and a general treatment of the Little Mandate. Because readers might be interested in obtaining this information, I provide here some sources for finding material given in these deleted sections.

If you have picked up this present volume, you probably already know something of Catherine's life and spirituality, and wish to know more of her spiritual motherhood, which has never been treated before at any length. A fair amount of biographical material in this book, therefore, is connected to the main thesis of her spiritual maternity or is related especially to her relationship with several of her own spiritual directors. Although her wisdom in guiding others has its fountainhead in the grace and mystery of the inspiration of the Holy Spirit, what she learned from directors while under their guidance was certainly a significant factor in her future guidance of others. And, of course, she acquired wisdom from *all* the events of her life. Regarding other aspects of her life, we have her own autobiography, *Fragments of my Life,* and Lorie Duquin's *They Called Her the Baroness.* A chronology of her life is also given in the Appendix for those unfamiliar with her life.

Concerning the Russian roots of her spirituality, Catherine herself published extensively on this topic. Though Fr. Guglielmi originally provided a unique summary of the Russian roots of Catherine's spirituality, it was thought that the section could be repetitious for those already knowledgeable with Catherine's own books.[2]

---

2. Those who are unfamiliar with Catherine's books on her Russian roots may be interested in pursuing the following titles, for which full information is listed in the bibliography and "Recommended Reading" at the end of this book: *Bogoroditza: She Who Gave Birth to God; Lubov: The Heart of the Beloved; Molchanie: The Silence of God; My Russian Yesterdays; Poustinia: Christian Spirituality of the East for Western Man; Sobornost; Strannik: The Call to Pilgrimage for Western Man;* and *Urodivoi.*

Finally, those familiar with Catherine's spirituality have probably heard about her "Little Mandate." These are deep words that she believed the Lord spoke to her and that formed the very heart of her understanding of how Jesus wanted her to live the Gospel. I myself have published a trilogy on the Mandate, using mostly Catherine's own reflections. (Madonna House Publications has published this trilogy in one volume.)

Ever since her cause was opened, I, as the postulator, have received hundreds of letters from people, testifying to how Catherine's responses have profoundly influenced their lives. This is not the place to share such testimonies but simply to mention their existence, and that they further confirm that she was a "bearer of the Spirit" in our time to many, many people. The general letters in her books from which Fr. Guglielmi will be quoting—*Dear Bishop, Dear Father, Dear Sister, Dear Parents, Dear Seminarian, and Dearly Beloved*—are only a fraction of the thousands of personal letters she wrote as an expression of her spiritual maternity.

It is quite common that upon completing a dissertation, the dissertator becomes engulfed in assignments. This has happened to Fr. Guglielmi. But as I have dedicated my life to making Catherine—whom I consider one of the great women of the 20th century—better known, I have been extremely interested in trying to see that Fr. Guglielmi's study is published. I have helped with the editing, but the work is Fr. Guglielmi's. May this study of Catherine's spiritual maternity help to deepen your appreciation of the extraordinary gospel wisdom of her life and teaching.

Fr. Robert Wild, Combermere, ON

Preface

In the introduction to the first volume of *Dearly Beloved: Letters to the Children of My Spirit*, the editors wrote:

> Catherine de Hueck Doherty could be described in various ways: a pioneer for interracial justice in North America; a great lover of the poor; a woman of immense faith, capable of inspiring faith in others; a passionate lover of Christ; a powerful preacher of the Gospel without compromise. All these descriptions would be true. But just as various ingredients are mixed in a bowl, and bread is poured out which is more wonderful than each ingredient by itself, so all the various dimensions of Catherine's life resulted in a grace that was the harmonious blending of all others. She became, in the Russian sense of "Staritsa," a spiritual mother: she daily fed her children, in all their needs, with the bread of Gospel wisdom.[3]

Forged in the crucible of the cataclysmic and transforming events of the twentieth century, Catherine de Hueck Doherty was led by God from her beloved Russia to the West, where, carrying the seed of the spiritual fruit of Holy Russia and planted in the new soil of the Catholic Church, she would discover her vocation as lay apostle and spiritual mother.

The present book is confined to the aspect of spiritual theology, defined by Royo-Marin as "that part of sacred theology which, based on the principles of divine revelation and the experience of the saints, studies the organism of the supernatural life, explains the laws of its progress and development, and describes the process which souls are wont to follow from the beginning of the Christian life to the heights of perfection."[4]

My book, I believe, breaks new ground in its use of primary and secondary unpublished archival sources. Particularly important is Catherine's

3. Doherty, Editors' Introduction to *Dearly Beloved: 1956–1963.*
4. Royo-Marin and Aumann, *Theology of Christian Perfection,* xxi.

correspondence with her various spiritual directors, entries from her spiritual diaries, her spiritual poetry, and various meditations, staff letters, and talks to priests and other groups. These sources offer the reader a privileged glimpse into Catherine's understanding of the Gospel, her passionate relationship with God, and her equally passionate desire to make Christ known and loved everywhere.

In my use of these sources I attempt to demonstrate that Catherine was a contemporary "bearer of the Spirit" and spiritual mother for the twentieth century. She articulated the ancient tradition and made it intelligible for the modern age. Catherine recognized that she was living in an era of de-Christianization characterized by hedonism, materialism, and cultural narcissism; and she understood its cause—a turning away from God.

As Fr. Wild mentions in his foreword, my original manuscript contained a chapter on Catherine's Eastern Orthodox roots and spirituality. Though this section was considered unnecessary for inclusion here because Catherine herself published a number of books on Eastern spirituality,[5] I will offer a few brief remarks about these Eastern roots.

Before her death in 1985, whenever Catherine surveyed the world from her *poustinia* in the northern woods of Ontario, she might have seen a remarkable vision. After enduring the loss of her family, her wealth, her social status, her country, and two husbands; after witnessing firsthand the catastrophic events of World War I, the Bolshevik Revolution, the Great Depression and World War II; after experiencing the apparent failure of two beloved apostolates at Friendship House, with its attendant rejection by staff and clergy, and temptations to despair, and even to suicide—Catherine could only have marveled at what God had created through her. Her gaze might have rested upon a new and vibrant ecclesial community where laymen, laywomen, and priests lived together in the same community under the promises of poverty, chastity, and obedience.[6]

She could have seen the fruits of Holy Russia, blending harmoniously with the Western Catholic tradition in a colorful and living array of customs, religious rituals, worship, and prayer, in a community that "breathes

---

5. *Poustinia*; *Sobornost*; *Strannik*; *Molchanie*; *Urodivoi*. All available at Madonna House Publications.

6. John Paul II, "Address of His Holiness . . . Meeting with the Ecclesial Movements and the New Communities," 219–24. In his address, Pope John Paul II spoke of new movements or ecclesial communities, predominantly lay in nature, which the Holy Spirit has raised up as new and vital expressions of the church. Madonna House is one such expression.

with the two lungs" of Eastern and Western Christianity. This expression was used by Pope John Paul II to refer to the Eastern and Western traditions of the Church, especially as they complement and enrich one another. In an address to the Catholic bishops of Ukraine, he stated, "Here the Church breathes with the two lungs of the Eastern and Western traditions. Here there is a fraternal meeting between those who draw from the sources of Byzantine spirituality and those who are nourished by Latin spirituality. Here the deep sense of mystery which suffuses the holy liturgy of the Eastern Churches and the mystical succinctness of the Latin Rite come face to face and mutually enrich each other."[7] The same could be said about the liturgical and religious life at Madonna House where both Eastern and Western religious traditions blend to enrich the spiritual lives of the community.

Unfolding before her radiant blue eyes would be an intensely Catholic environment where the "People of the Towel and the Water"[8] were striving to live the Gospel without compromise. In short, Catherine could have seen that, at Madonna House, a small corner of the world was being "restored in Christ." In Combermere, Ontario, a new expression of the Church totally immersed in the Gospel had taken root under Catherine's maternal guidance. This ecclesial community was and is founded on the Little Mandate.

The Little Mandate is her particular vision of living the Gospel without compromise. This was her "word" to the spiritually darkened world of the twentieth century, a word that has eternal value because it is rooted in the Gospel of Jesus Christ. This was one of her contributions for leading souls "from the beginning of the Christian life to the heights of perfection."

No lengthy treatment of the Little Mandate is given here because sufficient explanations of this have already appeared in print.[9] However, an understanding of the Little Mandate is essential to any discussion of Catherine's vocation and teaching, and thus of her spiritual maternity. Therefore, because it is important to keep the Mandate in mind for the rest of the book, I offer a brief word about this dimension of Catherine's spirituality for those who may be unfamiliar with it.

7. Pope John Paul II, "Ecumenical Dialogue," 26.

8. This expression is drawn from John 13:4–5, 12–15, describing how Jesus, using a basin and towel, washed the feet of his disciples at the Last Supper, as an action his disciples should imitate to express their servanthood. Catherine borrowed the term to describe one aspect of the Madonna House vocation: lay apostles who, by fulfilling the duty of the moment with love, serve their neighbors and manifest the dignity of manual labor.

9. See, for example, Wild, *Journey To the Heart of Christ*, 19.

The Little Mandate is a brief text that summarizes the spirituality that Catherine Doherty lived and proclaimed, revealing a theological vision for living the Gospel without compromise. It is an invitation to embark upon a journey of faith, and to live what Catherine called the "spirituality of Nazareth." From 1928 to 1934, Catherine received brief inspirations in the form of "words of command" which may be described as inner promptings of the Spirit. At first, whenever Catherine opened a Bible, her eyes always fell upon the same Gospel text, "Go, sell what you possess, and give to the poor" (Matt. 19:21). Then another "word" came while she was riding a streetcar. She had been thinking about giving her possessions to the poor, and the words "directly" and "personally" came to her. These words were followed by others, though they usually seemed unrelated to whatever time, place, or activity in which she found herself. This happened over the course of several years.

Catherine submitted these "words" for discernment to men she trusted for their wisdom and spiritual maturity, men she regarded as her spiritual directors. This vision to live the Gospel without compromise in an inner city apostolate to the poor took hold of Catherine during this period of discernment. She maintained that "these are the 'words' of God that my soul heard through the following years. The Mandate is what made me leave all things and go to Portland Street in Toronto." [10] Although there were some minor differences in the text as Catherine shared and recorded it, here is the final version that she approved:

> Arise—go! Sell all you possess. Give it directly,
> personally to the poor. Take up My cross (their cross)
> and follow Me, going to the poor, being poor,
> being one with them, one with Me
> Little—be always little! Be simple, poor, childlike.
> Preach the Gospel with your life—without compromise!
> Listen to the Spirit. He will lead you.
> Do little things exceedingly well for love of Me.
> Love, love, love, never counting the cost.
> Go into the marketplace and stay with Me.
> Pray, fast. Pray always, fast.
> Be hidden. Be a light to your neighbor's feet.
> Go without fears into the depths of men's hearts.
> I shall be with you.

10. Doherty, "The Little Mandate," April 27, 1968.

Pray always. I will be your rest. [11]

These words conditioned and informed her whole life with the Lord, and no aspect of her spirituality can be understood without them.

The heart of the present book is Catherine's *spiritual motherhood*, which was not merely one of words. Catherine witnessed to the Gospel without compromise with her life in the "marketplace" of the human community. This was the "desert" for her—in the slums of Toronto and Harlem, and in other places where Friendship Houses were established. Her apostolate proclaimed that being a Catholic, or being "a religious," is not simply a matter of attending church services or routinely "saying prayers," or even performing good works; rather, it's a way of both doing and *being*.

By applying the Gospel to numerous concrete situations, circumstances, and human problems, she demonstrated that living the Gospel is not an abstraction but a way of life. Her insistence on fulfilling the duty of the moment teaches Christians in every walk of life that every task, every responsibility—however small, unimportant, or monotonous—can become an opportunity to "restore the world to Christ" and to grow in holiness, if accomplished for the love of God and neighbor.

A unique characteristic of Catherine's spiritual motherhood was its exercise within the context of a lay vocation. This book attempts to demonstrate that she was a pioneer in the lay apostolate. Heeding the calls of Pope Leo XIII in *Rerum Novarum* (1891) and Pius XI in *Quadragesimo Anno* (1931), and Pope Pius XII in *Mystici Corporis Christi* (1943), she accepted her responsibility as a member of the Mystical Body of Christ, and sought to implement these papal teachings through an apostolate of Catholic Action. She was very much a woman of the Church, implementing the vision of the century's great popes. Thirty years later the Second Vatican Council's *Decree on the Apostolate of Lay People* called upon Catholics to be a leaven in the world, that by bearing witness to Christ and living a holy life, they might sanctify the temporal order:

> It is the work of the Church to fashion men able to establish the proper scale of values on the temporal order and direct it towards God through Christ. Laymen ought to take on themselves, as their distinctive task, this renewal of the temporal order. Guided by the light of the Gospel and the mind of the Church, prompted by

11. Doherty, "The Mandate of God to Catherine," 996–97.

Christian love, they should act in this domain in a direct way and in their own specific manner. [12]

Catherine's Little Mandate extends a challenge and invitation to modern Christians to do just that, by living the Gospel within the context of their daily responsibilities.

Another legacy of Catherine's lay vocation was the founding of the Madonna House Apostolate—one expression of a new ecclesial community, alive with the spirit of the Gospel. John Paul II recognized that the Holy Spirit was raising up in the Church today new movements and ecclesial communities, mostly lay in nature:

> Today a new stage is unfolding before you: that of ecclesial maturity.
>
> In our world, often dominated by a secularized culture which encourages and promotes models of life without God, the faith of many is sorely tested and frequently stifled and dies. Thus we see an urgent need for powerful proclamation and solid, in-depth Christian formation. There is great need today for mature Christian personalities, conscious of their baptismal identity, of their vocation, and mission in the Church and in the world! There is a great need for living Christian communities! And here are the movements and the new ecclesial communities: they are the response, given by the Holy Spirit, to this critical challenge at the end of the millennium.
>
> Thanks to this powerful ecclesial experience, wonderful Christian families have come into being which are open to life, true "domestic churches," and many vocations to the ministerial priesthood and the religious life have blossomed, as well as new forms of lay life inspired by the evangelical counsels. You have learned in the movements and new communities that faith is not abstract talk, nor vague religious sentiment, but new life in Christ instilled by the Holy Spirit. [13]

Catherine was one of these "mature Christian personalities, conscious of their baptismal identity, of their vocation, and mission in the Church and in the world," whose primary vocation was to be the founder and spiritual mother of Madonna House. This new ecclesial community comprises laymen, laywomen, and priests, living a common life of asceticism ordered

---

12. Vatican Council II, *Decree on the Apostolate of Lay People,* no.7.

13. John Paul II, "Address . . . on the Occasion of the Meeting with the Ecclesial Movements and the New Communities," nos. 6 & 7.

to the pursuit of perfection; consecrated to God through sacred promises; following a daily horarium; and guided by the "rule" or spirit of the Little Mandate. Though Madonna House possesses these monastic accents, canonically it is defined as a Public Association of the Faithful. Nevertheless, this canonical form does not capture the full scope of its nature.

> A unique dimension of these communities was that people from other canonical states—bishops, priests, religious, and families— were also attracted to them. What the Church and theologians are saying is that people, whether consciously or unconsciously, were actually seeking *a new and life-giving experience of the Church.* That is why these communities never "fit" canonical forms, because the Holy Spirit was inspiring new models for Church life, which includes all the states of life. [14]

The apostolate Catherine founded offers the world, in the hiddenness of Nazareth, "a new and life-giving experience of the Church." No doubt, the canon law of the Church will expand these canonical forms to include these new models of the Church that the Holy Spirit is creating.

One of Catherine's contributions to spiritual theology was to quicken in the Christian heart the idea of the redemptive value of suffering. Catherine's entire life was a painful way of the cross. From her exile from Russia to her final departure from this world, her life was filled with rejection, persecution, misunderstanding, and loneliness. Catherine did not use these sufferings as an excuse for paralyzing self-pity but as a divine invitation and God-given opportunity to advance in holiness. Through faith, she saw everything in life in relation to God, and this perspective enabled her to take up these crosses and see in them "the kiss of Christ." This expression invites those who suffer to understand their pain as an embrace by the Crucified One, an invitation to walk more closely the path he trod. Catherine perceived this "kiss" as a special sharing in victimhood. The depth of this calling was unique in her life, but its essence may also be embraced by everyone with what Catherine called her Little Mandate from God.

The remaining chapters in this book are an in-depth treatment of how Catherine discovered her vocation both as a lay apostle and, within that context, in her call to spiritual motherhood. Chapter 1 presents a theological analysis of Catherine as *staritsa* and examines her contribution to spiritual motherhood in the context of the tradition of the desert mothers

14. Wild, "A Vision of the Whole," no. 3.

(*ammas*) and the spiritual mothers (*staritsy*) of nineteenth century Russia. This chapter also considers Catherine's qualities as a spiritual mother.

Chapters 2, 3, and 4 demonstrate how she first experienced spiritual guidance from priestly friends and skilled spiritual directors. Among them was Archbishop Neil McNeil of Toronto, to whom Catherine turned repeatedly as the father of her soul and who was the first to help Catherine discern her lay vocation. Father Paul Wattson, SA, of Graymoor nurtured Catherine's love for the poor, fostered her vocation as a Franciscan Tertiary, and supported her financially and spiritually throughout her first apostolate at Friendship House, Toronto.

Catherine's major spiritual directors—Fathers Henry Carr, C.S.B., Paul Hanley Furfey, and John Callahan—all contributed profoundly to her formation as a spiritual mother. Catherine saw in each of these priests a type of spiritual father or *staritz*, and understood her relationship with them as that of spiritual father to disciple. Under their direction, Catherine's natural and supernatural gifts for guiding others to Christian perfection was nurtured and encouraged, and Catherine embraced this vocation with greater confidence as well. Her example bears witness to the fact that spiritual direction is important in the spiritual lives of the laity as well as in those of priests and religious.

Chapter 5 shows how she began to respond to the Spirit's call to guide priests; and chapter 6 shows how she continued to fulfill this ministry to religious and laity, and especially to the members of the Madonna House Apostolate.

One of Catherine's unique contributions was her spiritual motherhood to priests. Catherine called this her "second vocation"—"My first love is God, and my second love is priests." [15] God gave Catherine a tremendous capacity to love priests, to nurture them spiritually, and to offer her life as a victim soul for them; she did not hesitate to undertake this ministry to priestly souls. Her contribution to them cannot be underestimated. Catherine's spiritual motherhood to priests was a factor in saving several vocations and in leading other priests to deeper holiness.

Catherine ministered to priests by affirming their dignity and their identity as *alter Christus* and spiritual father. In its Instruction, *The Priest: Pastor and Leader of the Parish Community*, the Congregation for the Clergy expressed the view that there has been a crisis of priestly identity in recent times, "deriving sometimes from an unclear theological understanding of

15. Doherty, "Weakness of the Priest," September 23, 1975.

the two ways of participating in the priesthood of Christ, and of 'secularizing' the clergy."[16]

For Catherine, there was no confusion. She understood the essential difference between the priesthood of the laity and the sacrament of ordination. She repeatedly affirmed the identity of the priest, and exhorted him to act from a grateful awareness of that dignity. She nurtured in priests a love for Christ, for prayer, and for holiness of life, inviting them to intimacy with Jesus Christ.

We will see that Catherine encouraged priests to unite their loneliness and sufferings with those of their divine Master. Reminding them that "the price of souls is high," she invited them repeatedly to take their assigned place "on the other side of the cross." Using every possible means available to her, Catherine encouraged priests to (1) kneel with Jesus in Gethsemani during times of loneliness and misunderstanding; (2) practice obedience to ecclesial authority even in the midst of difficult pastoral assignments; (3) maintain *sobornost* or unity with brother priests and the laity, whatever the personal cost; (4) embrace kenosis for the sake of their personal sanctification; and (5) engage in selfless pastoral charity.

Catherine's spiritual motherhood, through her writings, continues to offer priests a way of understanding their vocation and living out its radical demands. They will find Catherine's teaching a source of spiritual formation, encouragement, and maternal charity in the trials and difficulties they encounter in their priestly lives.

In his Post-Synodal Apostolic Exhortation, *Vita Consecrata*, Pope John Paul II spoke of those called to respond to Christ's invitation to live the Gospel in a more radical way. In the monastic tradition, these men and women were considered "bearers of the Spirit, . . .authentically spiritual men and women, capable of endowing history with hidden fruitfulness by unceasing praise and intercession, by spiritual counsels and works of charity."[17] In addition to living a radical Gospel life in imitation of Christ, their witness was intended to "transfigure the world and life itself" through a radical self-renunciation and a ceaseless search for God.[18]

Eastern Orthodox scholar Joseph J. Allen states that "since the Spirit *does* abide in the Church, it follows that there *will* be an ever-renewing form

---

16. Congregation of the Clergy, *The Priest*, August 4, 2002.

17. John Paul II, *Vita Consecrata*, 16.

18. Ibid.

of πνευματοφόροι [*pneumatophoroi*]—'bearers' or 'carriers' of the Spirit."[19] Catherine's formation and spirituality reveal that she may be considered one such contemporary "bearer of the Spirit." Her desire to live the Gospel without compromise was a response in faith to the call of God and her contribution to restoring the world to Christ. In addition, as a bearer of the Spirit in the twentieth century, Catherine sought to lead and form others in a radical Gospel life. One way she attempted to fulfill this goal was through her spiritual maternity.

19. Allen, *Inner Way*, 4.

Acknowledgments

The current work began as a doctoral dissertation that was completed in Rome, and I would not have been able to complete this book without kind assistance and support from many people. First, I would like to extend my gratitude to my former bishop, the Most Reverent William E. Lori, Archbishop of Baltimore, who offered me the opportunity to complete a doctoral degree in theology in 2002.

I am also indebted to my original dissertation director, Father Gabriel O'Donnell, OP, whose patient guidance and scholarly advice inspired me to pursue excellence and who challenged, encouraged, and supported this endeavor. Many thanks to the second reader at my doctoral defense, Fr. Paul Murray, OP, for his valuable insights, suggestions and encouragement to make Catherine de Hueck Doherty better known as a spiritual mother. I am indebted, also, to Monsignor Peter Vaccari and the Faculty of St. Joseph's Seminary in Yonkers, NY, for their support and encouragement.

This work would not have been possible without the professional assistance and expertise of Bonnie Staib, the former Archivist at the Madonna House Apostolate. Many thanks also go to Father Robert Wild, who revised and shortened the original dissertation, helping to make it suitable for publication. I am also indebted to the prayers and encouragement of the entire Madonna House community. Thanks also to Barbara Martire, Archivist for the Franciscan Friars of the Atonement in Garrison, NY, for her thoughtful suggestions.

My gratitude extends also to those who granted copyright permission to use their primary and secondary resources: the current Directors-General of the Madonna House Apostolate, Father David Linder, Susanne Stubbs, and Larry Klein; Michelle Sawyers, MLIS, Congregational Archivist at the General Archives of the Basilian Fathers in Toronto, ON; Shane Mac-Donald, Archives Technician on behalf of the American Catholic History

Acknowledgments

Research Center at the Catholic University of America in Washington, DC; and to Deb Eisenschenk, Administrative Assistant, Publishers of Liturgical Press.

Finally, I would like to thank Pickwick Publications for agreeing to publish this work so that the spiritual motherhood exercised by Catherine de Hueck Doherty might be better known.

PART I

Catherine's Growth
in Spiritual Maternity

CHAPTER I

Defining Spiritual Direction, Paternity, and Maternity in the Traditions

When Catherine was exercising her maternity, she was always living out the words she herself had received from the Lord, her Little Mandate. This chapter provides both a general traditional understanding of spiritual direction as a background to Catherine's practice of it and a brief treatment of spiritual fatherhood and motherhood in the traditions of the East and Russia. Catherine was widely read in spirituality, and without doubt she knew the classical definitions and practices very well. How *she herself practiced such traditions*, however, as with any spiritual genius, was unique and cannot simply be reduced to any one definition.

SPIRITUAL DIRECTION

One classic Western definition of spiritual direction can be our starting point: "Spiritual direction is the art of leading souls progressively from the beginning of the spiritual life to the height of Christian perfection."[1] Pascal Parente adds, "Spiritual direction may be defined as the guidance of souls towards Christian perfection."[2] It is clear from the letters of correspondence

1. Royo-Marin and Aumann, *Theology of Christian Perfection*, 521.

2. Parente, *Spiritual Direction*, 13.

between Catherine and her directors that progressive guidance in holiness of life was what Catherine was seeking from spiritual direction and what her directors strove to provide.

In spiritual direction, it is the Holy Spirit who acts through a human instrument as the principal director of souls. Thomas Dubay makes the point that spiritual direction "is the guiding of a person into a life truly under the dominion of the Holy Spirit, who is the primary director. It helps the directee to be more and more docile to the light and promptings of the divine Sanctifier, identifying impediments to this, as well as ways to overcome them, giving instruction and encouragement in living a life of virtue, and assisting the directee to advance on the path of prayer—the road to union with God."[3]

The Incarnation of Jesus Christ is our starting point for a Christological understanding of spiritual direction. Christ's baptism was an occasion for the self-revelation of the Trinity: when the Holy Spirit descended upon Christ, the Father described him as "my beloved Son." Anointed with the power of the Holy Spirit, Jesus embarked upon his mission as the divine Spiritual Director. He drew men and women to himself and formed them in the new law of his kingdom.

In training his disciples, Jesus entered their hearts, offered them knowledge of God, and led them to the Father. He loved them unconditionally. He prayed for them. He spoke his saving "word" to them through parables, dialogue, and discourses. He taught them virtue by his example of holiness. He took upon himself their sins and burdens, suffering with and for them. He discerned the presence of evil and showed them how to recognize and combat it. As the divine Master of souls, Christ imparted the grace of *metanoia* to his disciples, his spiritual children, and invited them to adopt a whole new way of seeing and hearing.

Then he commissioned them to speak and act in his name, so that through them, vivified and guided by the Holy Spirit, they could direct all humankind toward its eschatological goal of unity with the Father. One of the important distinctions here is that, whereas the human director "fosters" *metanoia*, the incarnate Son of God *effects* the grace of conversion. Christ's direction is efficacious in ways different from the rest of us.

The Incarnation teaches us that no aspect of human life, apart from sin, is excluded from God's love. "The invitation offered to all in the Incarnation is that we should live in communion with God and with one another

---

3. Dubay, *Seeking Spiritual Direction*, 32–33.

in such a way that the whole of life, including not only personal aspects but also economic, social, political and cultural structures and institutions, is shaped by the presence of God. It is an invitation and encouragement to us to fashion all dimensions of human life in such a way that they share in and reflect the life of God."[4]

This is a primary goal of spiritual direction—to bring every aspect of human life into submission to God's will and, by doing so, to advance the reign of God in this world. Even the innermost sanctuary of a man, consisting of his thoughts, is subject to spiritual direction, for the thoughts reveal the interior dispositions of his heart. Thus, through spiritual direction, every area of human life—interior and exterior—becomes an opportunity to progress in the perfection of charity.

This sanctification of the human person accomplished through spiritual direction takes place in the bosom of the Church—the continuing presence of Christ in the world. The Spirit of God vivifies the Church so she may act infallibly in her office of teaching, governing, and sanctifying. The Church exercises a spiritual motherhood as she directs souls to God. John XXIII described her as *Mater et Magistra*—Mother and Teacher:

> *Mother* and *Teacher* of all nations—such is the Catholic Church in the mind of her Founder, Jesus Christ; to hold the world in an embrace of love, that men, in every age, should find in her their own completeness in a higher order of living, and their ultimate salvation. She is "the pillar and ground of the truth." To her was entrusted by her holy Founder the twofold task of giving life to her children and of teaching them and *guiding them—both as individuals and as nations—with maternal care.* Great is their dignity, a dignity which she has always guarded most zealously and held in the highest esteem (emphases added).[5]

Through baptism, the Church brings to birth new sons and daughters in the Spirit and shares the life of God with them. She nourishes these children with spiritual food and drink in the Eucharist; she teaches them the word of God and sacred doctrine, that "the man of God may be complete, equipped for every good work" (2 Tim 3:17), and directs them to their supernatural end.

Scripture also speaks of ordinary men and women in the Church who, led by the Spirit of God (Rom 8:14), share in the common priesthood of

4. Lonsdale, "Towards a Theology," 314.
5. John XXIII, *Mater et Magistra*, 1.

the baptized and possess gifts for the building up of the Body of Christ (1 Cor. 12). "The Spirit dwells in the Church and in the hearts of the faithful, as in a temple. Guiding the Church in the way of all truth, and unifying her in communion and in the works of ministry, he bestows upon her varied hierarchic and charismatic gifts, and in this way directs her and adorns her with his fruits."[6] Among these fruits one finds the gifts of spiritual direction and, consequently, of spiritual motherhood and fatherhood.

SPIRITUAL FATHERHOOD

Spiritual direction in the early Christian East and in nineteenth-century Russia, while following the same goal, included other elements. People prepared for spiritual fatherhood or motherhood by becoming a disciple or spiritual child to a spiritual master who was more experienced in the spiritual life. Spiritual direction "will be reserved for the relationship between *one* master, informed and experienced in the ways of the spirit, and *one* disciple who wishes to profit from such knowledge and experience. The essential, the indispensable, condition for becoming someone's spiritual father is to first be spiritual oneself."[7]

Following the teaching of John Climacus and Symeon the New Theologian, the spiritual father may be described in the following ways: First, he is a *doctor* who acts as a "spiritual healer and physician" of souls. This image employs a therapeutic model: "Confession is like going to the hospital; the penance is a tonic to assist the patient in his recovery. Moreover, the spiritual child reveals to his father not only his sins but more generally his 'thoughts' (*logismoi*), long before they have led to outward acts."[8]

Second is *counselor*—the spiritual father can also heal the soul by his counsel—that is, by his words—and even by his silent presence. "The word of the spiritual father is a word of power, saving, regenerating. While healing by his speech, the spiritual father may also heal by his silence, that is, simply by virtue of his presence."[9]

Third, he is *intercessor*: the spiritual father heals the soul by his prayers of intercession for the spiritual child, an intercession that may continue

---

6. Vatican Council II, *Lumen Gentium (Dogmatic Constitution on the Church)*, 352.

7. Hausherr, *Spiritual Direction*, 12.

8. Ibid., xii–xiii.

9. Ibid., xiii.

"even after his death."[10] Fourth, he is *mediator*—the spiritual father is a friend of God with "direct inspiration by the Holy Spirit. The spiritual father is the king's friend, who can therefore gain the royal favor on behalf of others. The mediation works in both directions: the spiritual father not only represents us to God but equally represents God to us."[11]

On this point, John Climacus compares the spiritual father to Moses with his hands outstretched before God: "Those of us who wish to get away from Egypt, to escape from Pharaoh, need some Moses to be our intermediary with God, that those led by him may cross the sea of sin and put to flight the Amalek of the passions. Those of us who have given themselves up to God, but imagine that they can go forward without a leader, are surely deceiving themselves."[12]

Fifth, the director is *sponsor*. The spiritual father takes upon himself the responsibility and burden of the directees' temptations and struggles. "The spiritual father is more particularly an image or ikon of Christ the Good Shepherd, who carried the lost sheep on his shoulders and laid down his life for the flock. An essential characteristic of the spiritual father is *sympatheia*, 'compassion,' in the full sense of suffering with and for others."[13] Symeon, a spiritual father, also emphasized "the image of the father begetting children, or even of the mother conceiving and bearing them," and he regards the spiritual father as an apostle.[14]

SPIRITUAL MOTHERHOOD

The earliest witness to the formal practice of spiritual maternity in the Church is found in the tradition of desert monasticism. In Eastern monasteries of the fourth to the sixth centuries, holy women served as spiritual guides and were known as *ammas*. Sr. Donald Corcoran, OSB, describes them in this way: "The desert fathers/mothers were the first Christian monks and nuns who, from the fourth to the sixth century, peopled the desert and wilderness regions of Egypt, Palestine, and Syria. People were drawn to the desert to find an 'elder,' an accomplished ascetic and spiritual

10. Ibid., xiv–xv.

11. Ibid., xvi–xviii.

12. Climacus, *The Ladder of Divine Ascent*, 75.

13. Ibid., xxiii–xxvi.

14. Ibid., xxvii.

teacher capable of leading other persons to a greater experience of God."[15] Laura Swan, OSB, adds, "An *amma* or *abba* was someone seasoned in the ascetic life who was known to have reached a level of maturity and wisdom, and had experience in teaching by example, exhortation, story, and instruction."[16]

Hausherr offers a more general description: "*Ammas*—this is what spiritual women were called or, according to a variant, 'spiritual mothers.'"[17] The title *amma* refers to one's ability to become a spiritual mother, not necessarily to the role of abbess in a monastery for women.[18]

There are exceptions, however. Some *ammas* were also spiritual mothers and founders of monasteries for women—for example, Melania the Elder and her grand-daughter, Melania the Younger.[19] Soler writes, "Because she could be 'spiritual' (a bearer of the Spirit) a female ascetic could guide others, and as such could be called 'mother' or 'amma.' This title corresponded to the title 'father' or 'abba' and indicated aptitude to be a spiritual mother."[20]

Palladius describes the rise of monasticism in Egypt, Syria, Palestine and Asia Minor, and provides a biographical sketch of sixty holy men and women. Among these, Palladius writes of "saintly women," (literally, "manly women"), whom he identifies as spiritual mothers equal to men in their successful practice of virtue.[21] The *Apopthegamata Patrum* names three spiritual mothers as well: Sara, Syncletica, and Theodora.[22]

There are others, such as Mary of Egypt, a repentant sinner who spent forty years in the Egyptian desert.[23] The following passage, describing the encounter between the monk Zossima and *Amma* Mary of Egypt, is instructive for our understanding of spiritual motherhood.

> [Zossima] knelt down and asked her to give him the customary blessing. She also knelt down. So they both remained on the ground asking one another for a blessing. After a long time the

15. Corcoran, "Spiritual Guidance," 446.

16. Swan, *Forgotten Desert Mothers*, 11.

17. Hausherr, *Spiritual Direction*, 277.

18. Ibid.

19. Peterson, *Handmaids of the Lord*, 28.

20. Soler, "The Desert Mothers," 31.

21. Palladius, *The Lausiac History*, 3–4, 117, 203.

22. Ward, *Sayings of the Desert Fathers*, ix–xi.

23. Peterson, *Handmaids of the Lord*, 27.

woman said to Zossima, "Father Zossima, it is proper for you to give the blessing and say the prayer, for you have the dignity of the office of a priest, and for many years you have stood at the holy table and offered the sacrifice of Christ." These words threw Zossima into greater dread. He trembled and was covered with a sweat of death. But at last, breathing with difficulty, he said to her, "O *Mother in the spirit*, [emphasis added] it is plain from this insight that all your life you have dwelt with God and have nearly died to the world. It is plain above all that grace is given you since you called me by my name and recognized me as a priest though you have never seen me before. But since grace is recognized not by office but by gifts of the Spirit, bless me, for God's sake, and pray for me out of the kindness of your heart." So the woman gave way to the wish of the old man, and said, "Blessed is God who cares for the salvation of souls." Zossima answered, "Amen," and they both rose from their knees.[24]

Amma Mary inquired about the reason for Zossima's visit and the state of the Church throughout the empire. Zossima responded,

"By your prayers, Mother, Christ has given lasting peace everywhere. But hear the request of an unworthy monk and pray to the Lord for the whole world and for me, a sinner, that my wandering through the desert should not be without fruit." She answered him, "It is only right, Father Zossima, that you who have the office of a priest should pray for me and for all; but we must be obedient so I shall willingly do what you bid of me." With these words, she turned to the East and raising her eyes to heaven and stretching up her hands she began to pray moving her lips in silence, so that almost nothing intelligible could be heard. So Zossima could not understand anything of her prayer.[25]

According to Mary Forman, OSB, this text illustrates the dynamic of spiritual motherhood in the life of Mary of Egypt: "Twice in this account Zossima the priest 'father' calls Mary 'mother,' that is, *amma*, because she is a 'Mother in the spirit.' Of significance in the story is the fact that the normal cultural expectation that a Christian woman would seek a blessing of a priest is reversed: instead Zossima the 'father' asks a blessing of the 'mother.'"[26]

24. Ward, *Sayings of the Desert Fathers*, 31.

25. Ibid.

26. Forman, "Desert Ammas," 189.

Note, too, that Mary demonstrated a gift of discernment when she recognized Zossima as a priest, although his identity was unknown to her. Zossima acknowledged Mary as a spiritual mother bearing gifts in the Spirit and asked her to pray for him and "for the whole world." Forman comments: "This capacity to cooperate with the grace of the Spirit, making of woman a channel of grace to others, is the reason Mary and other women of spiritual strength were called *ammas*. These women exercised a spiritual maternity on a par with the spiritual paternity of the *abbas*; thus they could transmit spiritual doctrine with the same right as the monks. The only thing they could not do was absolve sins sacramentally."[27]

Forman describes the *ammas* as "midwives" because they were bearers of the Spirit: "These women, in their spiritual direction and in their generous sharing either of physical wealth or the wealth of their experience and giftedness, were able to midwife Christ's birth in those whom they served."[28] They are called "midwives of wisdom" because they possessed the gift of discernment—from the Latin verb, *sapere*—"to discern" and "to be wise."[29]

Characteristics of the Spiritual Mother

Five fundamental roles of a spiritual father were identified earlier—doctor, counselor, intercessor, mediator and sponsor. *Amma* Theodora broadens Hausherr's list and identifies the qualities that indicate a spiritual maturity commensurate with the role of spiritual mother.[30] "Theodora's list basically corresponds with the elements required by all early monasticism, especially in Egypt and Palestine."[31] The qualities required of a spiritual father and mother are interchangeable; many overlap and reinforce each other. According to *Amma* Theodora, a spiritual mother should be "a stranger to the desire for domination, vain-glory, and pride" or positively, one must be humble.[32] Rather, a spirit of respect and gentleness ought to characterize her relationship with souls. She must acknowledge herself as a redeemed

---

27. Ibid.
28. Ibid., 193.
29. Ibid., 196.
30. Soler, "Desert Mothers," 33.
31. Ibid.
32. Ward, *Sayings of the Desert Fathers*, 83.

sinner who must rely on God's grace to guide others. Likewise, "the spiritual father must be a saint who calls himself a sinner."[33]

Amma Mary of Egypt captured this quality in her encounter with Zossima. She affirmed his dignity and the power of his priestly blessing and prayer before she agreed to grant his request for her blessing and prayers; and at the same time, she acknowledged her own need for prayer.

A spiritual mother should possess a spirit of detachment from worldly possessions, gifts, and honors.[34] This quality serves to maintain the freedom of the spiritual mother to guide the soul with detachment—to say what is necessary for the soul's growth in holiness. This freedom of heart will also allow the spiritual mother to offer her directee spiritual friendship—"the authentic friendliness of disinterested love."[35]

A spiritual mother should possess self-mastery and control of her passions.[36] This is the characteristic of the genuine ascetic who has attained a degree of *apatheia* by conquering the disorderly passions. In this way, the spiritual mother can offer the soul an example of forbearance and moderation. A spiritual mother should be patient in dealing with others.[37] This patience and gentleness reflect the divine attributes of mercy and kindness, and allow the spiritual mother to model these virtues for the good of the soul.[38]

A spiritual mother should have a reputation for holiness and experience in the spiritual life.[39] "This experience does not only come from exceptional graces. It comes first from a familiarity with temptation and trial. A father not himself purified by fire could easily lead others to despair."[40] The spiritual father or mother will have proficiency in facing and overcoming the trials that constitute the spiritual life. In this way, he or she may offer the soul encouragement and hope.

The spiritual mother should be "full of concern, and a lover of souls."[41] This charity for souls motivates all that the spiritual father and

33. Hausherr, *Spiritual Direction*, 68.

34. Ward, *Sayings of the Desert Fathers*, 83.

35. Soler, "Desert Mothers," 34.

36. Ibid.

37. Ibid.

38. Louf, "Spiritual Fatherhood," 52.

39. Soler, "Desert Mothers," 34.

40. Louf, "Spiritual Fatherhood," 43.

41. Ward, *Sayings of the Desert Fathers*, 84.

mother do and say with regard to their disciples. Hausherr adds charity and discernment as the primary qualities for the spiritual mother.[42] The spiritual mother is someone who loves God and neighbor and who makes this love the paramount quest of life. Moreover, "it is beyond question that it is charity or the reputation of charity that attracts disciples, not only average sinners seeking a remedy for their ills, but the saints themselves."[43] Hausherr understands the practice of patience, gentleness, kindness, and humility as ways in which the spiritual mother exercises charity.

Discernment or *diakrisis* enables the spiritual mother to detect the activity of evil spirits, to understand the origin of dreams, thoughts, and motives. This gift helps the spiritual son or daughter to grow in self-knowledge and to avoid the snares set by the devil. "Spiritual direction is merely the discernment of spirits put into practice for the profit of those being directed."[44] Hausherr states that "there were *degrees in the gift of diakrisis: kardiognosis* (knowledge of the heart); and *diakrisis*, spiritual insight," a type of clarity of vision that can sometimes foresee future events correctly.[45] The former is a pure gift of God given to some spiritual mothers, and the latter is the fruit of purification and *apatheia*.[46]

The monk Zossima affirmed that both *kardiognosis* and *diakrisis* were gifts possessed by *Amma* Mary of Egypt. The former was evident when she recognized him as a priest: "it is plain that grace is given you since you called me by my name and recognized me as a priest."[47] The latter was demonstrated when Zossima said, "it is plain from this *insight* [emphasis added] that all your life you have dwelt with God and have nearly died to the world."[48]

Hausherr adds that the spiritual mother must be able to speak a word that is clear, effective, and suited to the spiritual needs of her spiritual children.[49] That word is the fruit and expression of charity. Soler understands this to be "the gift of saying or doing the exact thing that will stir

42. Hausherr, *Spiritual Direction*, 58.

43. Ibid.

44. Ibid., 77.

45. Ibid.

46. Ibid.,92.

47. Ward, *Sayings of the Desert Fathers*, 42.

48. Ibid.

49. Hausherr, *Spiritual Direction*, 96.

the disciple to action at the right moment."[50] Burton-Christie states that "*The Sayings of the Desert Fathers* emerged and gained currency as words of power, life, and salvation addressed to particular persons in concrete situations."[51] To this end, the desert fathers often applied Scripture to the daily life circumstances of their spiritual children. Graham Gould writes that "interpretation of Scripture is part of the responsibility of the Abba as spiritual father and instructor of his disciples."[52]

Burton-Christie outlines a schema for understanding the diverse literary expressions found in the *Sayings*. Drawing from the *Vita Antonii* of Athanasius, Burton-Christie argues that the *Sayings* take three forms: exhortation, exposition and eulogy.[53] Exhortation includes "'salvation sayings' consisting of a variety of personal responses related directly to the needs of an individual. In some cases, these concrete and personal words were adapted gradually to meet the needs of an expanding monastic community."[54] Exposition clarifies and further expands upon the meaning of a word.[55] Eulogy "takes the form of expressions of the praiseworthy qualities and accomplishments of the heroes of the desert movement," with a view to imitation.[56] We shall see how these elements were characteristic of Catherine's spiritual maternity.

Benedicta Ward affirms that the desert mothers broadly applied Scripture in guiding their children with a word of salvation: "The language of the writings of the desert was so formed by the meditation on the scriptures that it is almost impossible to say where quotation ends and comments begin."[57] The word emerged from the heart of the *amma*, who was taught by God in the solitude of her monastic cell, and was intended to feed the disciple with the scriptural "bread of life."[58]

For this reason, Ward describes this "word"—regardless of its form— as a "sacrament": "The abba did not give 'spiritual direction': if asked, he would give a 'word' which would become a sacrament to the hearer. The

---

50. Soler, "Desert Mothers," 34.

51. Burton-Christie, *The Word in the Desert*, 78.

52. Gould, "Note on the *Apophthegmata Patrum*," 135.

53. Ibid., 91.

54. Ibid.

55. Ibid.

56. Ibid., 92.

57. Ward, "Spiritual Direction in the Desert Fathers," 64–65.

58. Ibid., 65.

'word' was not to be discussed or analyzed or disputed in any way; at times, it was not even understood; but it was to be memorized and absorbed into life, as a sure way towards God."[59]

Duties of the Spiritual Mother

According to Hausherr, the qualities of a spiritual mother involve a "practical application governed by a very important principle, that of the aim to be followed, namely the disciple's spiritual growth."[60] This practical application may be called the duties of the spiritual mother, which include the following.

The spiritual mother must willingly take up her role when asked to by someone who seeks spiritual guidance. Frequently, there is a temptation to flee from the responsibilities of spiritual motherhood, but Hausherr insists that their acceptance is a sign of charity for souls, and this acceptance must be accompanied by a profound humility and trust in God.[61] The spiritual mother must pray for her spiritual children.[62] Prayer is necessary for the spiritual mother to practice the virtues that will edify her spiritual children and to obtain the desired spiritual profit for them. This prayer is a grave obligation under the law of charity: "The Desert Fathers had the care of souls, and to have care of souls means devoting oneself to this spiritual welfare as to one's own salvation; it means giving them a privileged place in the unending supplication addressed to God by one's entire life transformed into prayer."[63] The spiritual mother must carry the burdens of her spiritual disciples.[64]

> Surely this is the most important thing: to take on oneself the responsibility for the other's eternal salvation. This is the spiritual father: a man who takes his children's peace and progress in virtue so to heart that he does not hesitate to take upon himself, as far as he can, their present with its worries of the moment, and their future with the need to discern for them the will of God.[65]

59. Ibid., 63–66.
60. Hausherr, *Spiritual Direction*, 123.
61. Ibid., 125.
62. Ibid., 129.
63. Ibid., 131.
64. Ibid., 141.
65. Ibid., 146, 149.

The spiritual mother must be a teacher of the souls under her guidance, with a view to generating virtue in them.[66] The spiritual mother accomplishes this by modeling the virtues in her own life, especially charity, and also by teaching spiritual doctrine.[67] The latter has often taken the form of a "word" or *rhema*, given in response to the disciple's request.[68] This word, as we have seen, was intended to touch the heart of the disciple: "At first the questioner sought an active word charged with mysterious power which, well received, touches the heart and opens a way by which new life may burst forth. Reduced to its simplest expression, it proclaims and grants salvation, and it does so with such sovereign might that it seems to come from God himself"[69]

Hausherr augments our understanding of this vocation by summarizing the qualities and responsibilities of spiritual motherhood:

> All the workers employed by Providence for this great work—from the Word Incarnate and the Holy Spirit to the most Blessed Virgin Mary and holy Church, to the last of the occasional benefactors—all those who transmit the divine life to us and who cause us to have this life more abundantly by making the Father known to us, by making us believe in his love, by trusting the fulfillment of his fatherly design, by making us love everything he loves, by making us find in this faith, this love, the peace of God and the joy of Christ. In a word, all those who contribute to creating Christ in us or reforming us according to the model of Christ, partake of divine Fatherhood and deserve analogically the name of father and mother according to the Spirit, because they make us better children of God.[70]

The Staritsa Tradition in Holy Russia

The fourth-century desert mothers of the East were the inspiration for another group of holy women, known as the spiritual mothers of Holy Russia. While it is difficult to establish a direct historical connection between the fourth-century *ammas* and the holy women of Russia, Hausherr claims that

66. Ibid., 284.

67. Ibid., 286.

68. Louf, "Spiritual Fatherhood," 38.

69. Ibid., 38–39.

70. Hausherr, *Spiritual Direction*, 322–23.

"the tradition of spiritual fatherhood and motherhood retained its full significance throughout the Byzantine era, while from Byzantium it spread to the Slav Orthodox world."[71]

Kontzevitch confirms this and maintains that there were "direct contacts with Byzantium on the one hand, maintained by the arrival of the Greeks in Russia and, on the other hand, by Russians traveling to the East. Some travelers were drawn to Palestine, others went to Constantinople."[72] These Russian "travelers" to Palestine carried the tradition of the desert mothers to their country.

For this reason, there are clear parallels between the earlier prototypes and the spiritual women who emerged in Russia during the nineteenth century as *staritsy*. The two bore similar characteristics—a passionate search for God, renunciation of wealth, prayer, fasting, a desire for solitude—as well as concern for the poor. Both groups attracted followers and spiritual children who sought guidance from their wisdom. Russian studies scholar Brenda Meehan states that the holy women of Russia "followed the desert ideal of Eastern Christianity, seeing in the forests of northern Russia the symbolic equivalent of the Egyptian and Syrian deserts, and referring to a hermitage as a desert (*poustinia*)."[73] In her instructions to novices, the *staritsa* Abbess Thaisia extolled the desert mothers' way of life and practice of virtue as worthy of emulation.[74]

The *staritsa* tradition in Russia embraced abbesses, nuns, and holy laywomen.[75] Among the ranks of the spiritual mothers were both virgins and married women who embraced the Orthodox monastic life following the deaths of their husbands.[76] For example, Margarita Tuchkov (1781–1852) was happily married for six years until her husband's death. When her only child also died, she turned to God more fervently, served the poor and grief-stricken, and eventually established a religious community for women, for whom she became a spiritual mother.[77]

Another example is Mother Angelina (1809–1890), who was born into an aristocratic family in St. Petersburg. After her husband of thirty-four

71. Ibid., x.

72. Kontzevitch, *The Acquisition of the Holy Spirit*, 120.

73. Meehan, *Holy Women of Russia*, 49.

74. Abbess Thaisia, *Letters to a Beginner*, 30–32.

75. Kontzevitch, *The Acquisition of the Holy Spirit*, 70.

76. Meehan, *Holy Women of Russia*, 2.

77. Ibid., 33.

years died, she tired of worldly wealth and privilege, embraced the monastic life, and became mother superior to a women's religious community.

Another *staritsa*, Anastasia Lugacheva, ministered to the spiritual needs of others outside of the monastic life. Her vocation as spiritual mother involved a life of solitude in the Russian forest. These and other women of Holy Russia lived ordinary lives but felt called to embrace Russian monasticism, which was considered the highest ideal for those seeking perfection. As they grew in charity and humility, each of them attracted spiritual children and became an "eldress" (*staritsa*).[78] Catherine, being Russian, but having lived most of her adult life as a Roman Catholic, would have been influenced by both these traditions—the desert *ammas* and the *staritsy* of nineteenth-century Russia.

78. An outstanding modern Russian staritsa is Mother Maria Skobtsova (1891–1945). Cf. *Mother Maria Skobtsova.*

PART II

Catherine's Formation through Her Experience of Spiritual Direction

CHAPTER 2

Archbishop Neil McNeil, Father Paul Wattson, SA, and Father Henry Carr

Chapters 2, 3, and 4 will focus on the development of Catherine's spiritual maternity through her personal experience of spiritual direction and priestly friendships. We will examine several major spiritual directors that Catherine enjoyed over the course of her life, and we will study the influences of these priestly relationships on her formation as a spiritual mother.

Although Catherine did not consciously set out to become a spiritual mother or director—her early writings indicate that she thought this would be presumptuous and proud—we can trace how God prepared her for this aspect of her vocation. One way was through her experience of being a spiritual daughter to various spiritual fathers or *abbas* (in Russian, *staritsy*). What she learned about the art of directing people from them would prove valuable in the future when she began to exercise a similar ministry for others.

The traditions briefly outlined in the previous chapter were little known in the Christian life of North America in the twentieth century. Thus, it is safe to assume that Catherine's understanding and belief in the importance of spiritual direction came mostly from her Russian tradition. Catherine was convinced that spiritual direction was necessary for the interior life. For most of her adult life, she sought out and had spiritual directors. Here, it is necessary only to refer to four main directors and the precepts she learned from them that most probably became ingredients in her own practice of spiritual maternity.

CATHERINE'S THREE EARLIEST DIRECTORS

Catherine first learned the value and importance of seeking spiritual guidance from her parents, who taught her that the bishop is the spiritual father of the soul. They encouraged her to go to him whenever she needed direction in her life.[1] When Catherine lived in Toronto, she began a filial relationship with Archbishop Neil McNeil, who supported her initial efforts to begin a new apostolate to the poor. Even though Archbishop McNeil was not Catherine's spiritual director in the technical sense, our study would be incomplete without mentioning his influence in her vocation. He served as a spiritual father to Catherine, and she continued to consult him with on issues pertaining to her personal, spiritual, and apostolic life. Archbishop McNeil was a continuous influence and support for Catherine until his death in 1934.

Father Paul Wattson, SA, of Graymoor was the first real spiritual father Catherine had in North America, and probably the first in her life. Their correspondence reveals his enormous influence on Catherine. He was the only person she ever addressed as "My dearly beloved Father," often signing her letters with "your daughter" or "your loving daughter." Father Paul was her spiritual father in a way the others were not. He supported Catherine's apostolate financially, nurtured her vocation as a Third Order Franciscan, and was a source of emotional and spiritual support during a difficult period in her life. This chapter will explore his influence upon and contribution to her development as a spiritual mother.

Father Henry Carr, CSB, is also included in this chapter. He was a profound guide for her in the early years of her Toronto apostolate and an unwavering support in the trials of misunderstanding that culminated in her having to leave Toronto. Father Paul Hanly Furfey (Chapter 3) and Father John Callahan (Chapter 4) are especially important for this study because they formed Catherine at a time when she was becoming increasingly aware of her own vocation to spiritual motherhood. By offering her a relationship of spiritual father and daughter, they helped Catherine to

---

1. Doherty, *Strannik*, 46.

discern her vocation of spiritual motherhood and encouraged her to embrace it.

As elders in the spiritual life, they taught Catherine the way of charity, humility, detachment, and *apatheia*, as well as the arts of discernment and prayer. Under their guidance, Catherine learned to live out the Little Mandate and to teach others to do so. By becoming a spiritual daughter, she matured into spiritual motherhood. Catherine engaged in these relationships primarily by means of written correspondence, because she was often separated geographically from her directors. The unpublished letters of direction preserved in the Madonna House Archives will serve as the primary source of information.

Catherine learned the art of spiritual motherhood from the priests who were more experienced in the spiritual life, as a disciple would learn from his spiritual master. For Catherine, however, spiritual direction was more fluid than a simple one-to-one relationship between director and directee. She had only one spiritual director at a time, but she freely sought spiritual advice from several sources at once. In some cases, when one spiritual director could not offer her the help that she needed, she consulted another priest and engaged in correspondence with more than one priest at the same time.

For example, in the 1930s, Catherine had correspondence with her spiritual father, friend and confidante, Father Paul Wattson, SA of Graymoor, and with Father Henry Carr, C.S.B., who had been appointed as spiritual director of Friendship House. St. Teresa of Avila did much the same thing. Catherine hungered for a word of holiness and direction and sought it from every available good source.

Father Paul Wattson, SA of Graymoor

Father Paul Wattson was a former Episcopal priest with an interest in promoting unity between the Catholic Church and the American Episcopal Church. To that end, he co-founded, with Lurana White—an Episcopalian Sister who shared his vision—the Society of the Atonement at Garrison, New York, and known by the popular name "Graymoor" a few years before his reception in the Catholic Church. His cause for canonization was opened on September 22, 2015, and is progressing.

Catherine first met Father Paul in 1926 while working as a lecturer for the Catholic Near East Welfare Association where Father Paul was on the board of directors.[2] He was interested in her Russian Orthodox background and invited her to visit his friary at Graymoor. For her part, Catherine was deeply impressed by what she saw in the Franciscan Friars of the Atonement. She was very attracted to their Franciscan spirit of poverty and simplicity, and the ecumenical orientation of their apostolate. "Father Paul's devotion to Saint Francis of Assisi reminded Catherine of how much she had admired that saint during her school days in Egypt. In a quiet Graymoor chapel, Catherine knelt before the altar as Father Paul received her into the Third Order of Saint Francis, which meant she would try to live the Franciscan spirit as a lay person."[3]

Catherine had much in common with Father Paul in his vision of Episcopal-Roman unity. Like him, she was poor, prophetic, misunderstood, and before her time: a pioneer in the lay apostolate. Like him, she had a dream in which laymen, laywomen, and priests could live together in harmony and live the Gospel without compromise. Like him, she suffered for her dream and could only rely on trust in God. Catherine described her vision as "a dream dreamt in God." Father Paul was a solid contributor to missionaries all over the world and especially to those most in need, and Catherine's apostolate was one such recipient of his generosity and support.

Catherine saw in Father Paul of Graymoor a prophetic priest, enlightened by the Holy Spirit, filled with divine wisdom and apostolic courage, boldly confident in God's providence, passionately devoted to the salvation of souls, ecumenically sensitive, and hard-working. In these respects, Catherine regarded Father Paul as a type of *staretz*, similar to those she had encountered in the monasteries of her beloved Russia. Her long association with Father Paul of Graymoor and empathy with the spirit of the Friars of the Atonement nurtured her own spiritual development, as well as the spirit of her lay apostolate. Father Paul nurtured her during the infancy years of her lay apostolate, which laid the foundation for Catherine's emerging vocation as spiritual mother. The two were inseparably linked—Catherine's lay apostolate and spiritual motherhood—as it was within the context of her lay apostolate that she discovered and exercised her spiritual motherhood.

In the following selections from key letters between Catherine and Father Paul Wattson, SA, it is important to note again that Father Paul was always addressed as "Dear and Beloved Father" and Father Paul's to Catherine are addressed to "My dear Daughter." In a letter addressed to the Most

2. Duquin, *They Called Her the Baroness*, 98.

3. Ibid.

Reverend Pascal Robinson, Papal Nuncio to Ireland, Father Paul described Catherine as "my very dear personal friend, as well as spiritual daughter."[4]

Her correspondence with Father Paul reveals a healthy spiritual relationship. She related to Father Paul as a man of God who was could assist her at various levels, and she was confident of his willingness to serve the cause of her apostolate. Catherine expressed an almost child-like confidence in her relationship with Father Paul, which seemed to call forth a generous response from him. Father Paul nearly always complied with Catherine's requests to write letters on her behalf unless there was a prudent reason for not doing so, which he would then gently explain to her.

Father Paul had the prophetic grace to understand the need for the lay apostolate in the Catholic Church. His various apostolic endeavors prompted Catherine to share with him her own understanding of the growing lay participation in the mission of the Church. She wrote:

> As I see it, the Lay Apostolate is a free, modern, pliant, humane organization going out into the highways and byways of the world where neither priests nor nuns have access, working in an original fashion to combat the great new menace of atheism, keeping to the sound old idea of the Church which is that any active apostolate, no matter how new or startling in its methods, has its roots in Christ, and is a channel for His grace, which insists as a first step a great impetus towards personal sanctification. Built on the foundation of personal sanctification, there is obedience to the precepts and commands of the Church and its Hierarchy. The lay apostle can be the mobile son of the Church, ever ready for action, ever prompt for emergency.[5]

Because Father Paul understood Catherine's vocation and inner desire for holiness, he was able to write such letters as the following to the Hierarchy in support of her apostolate. It also testifies to an aspect of her character important for our study: she humbly submitted herself to spiritual guidance.

> It seems to me that God has given her a real apostolate to the Communists. She possesses a grasp and understanding of the red propaganda quite beyond that of the ordinary student of bolshevism. Ever since she came to America she has been a public lecturer on the subject as well as a publicist writer. If she has been

4. Wattson, letter to Pascal Robinson, June 7, 1937.
5. Doherty, letter to Father Wattson, November 15, 1935.

heretofore on the subject a "free lance," nevertheless she has shown a disposition to be under direction and ecclesiastical control. Otherwise why should she seek to submit herself and her associates to the rule of the Third Order of St. Francis and at the same time to seek to submit herself to a spiritual director? Some have called her proud, but in reality I regard her as a very humble woman, not hesitating to scrub the floors and to do the most menial tasks in ministering to the poor, to spend and be spent in the service of humanity.[6]

In her letters, Catherine often expressed her expectations and hopes from the leadership of Father Paul: "You beloved Father, who in your life exemplifies uncompromising Christianity, you who are the image of St. Francis who was never afraid—who better than you in the Lamp [Fr. Paul's newspaper] which implies 'Light' is qualified to start this attack on the world of selfishness and greed, atheism and paganism. I can see you receiving the spirit of the little known company of Tertiaries throughout our world—and leading them through the uncompromising Christianity of our Holy Father St. Francis, to the conquest of the world for Christ!"[7]

Though Catherine was speaking quite personally to Father Paul, well aware of his personal struggles and history in living the Gospel without compromise, and the persecution and suffering he endured because of his commitment, she was also addressing her comments to all priests. Catherine sought and expected courageous and uncompromising spiritual leadership from all priests. He is the one who is ordained to lift high the standard of Christ—to be a "Lamp"—a "Light" in the world to shine the truth of Christ upon a world in the grip of greed, selfishness, and paganism. In short, Catherine was saying to Father Paul, and to all priests, generally: "Be real! Be true to the vocation Christ has given you!" She learned from the example of Father Paul what a true priest is and could be, and she began, in a small measure, to exercise spiritual motherhood on his behalf.

In a brief article published by *Restoration* in 1951 after Father Paul's death, Catherine summarized what Father Paul Wattson, SA, of Graymoor meant to her.

> How can one book exhaust CHARITY, WHOSE OTHER NAME IS LOVE? Father Paul was a FIRE OF CHARITY, A TORCH OF LOVE that lighted this dark world to its farthest corners.

6. Wattson, letter to Archbishop McNeil, August 26, 1936.
7. Catherine, letter to Father Wattson, SA, January 13, 1937.

While he was living, he would be one of the foremost exponents of the sublime doctrine of the Mystical Body of Christ. I remember a trip we made together from Garrison to New York City, in the days when no one talked much of the Mystical Body of Christ. Father Paul was explaining to me the oneness of all men in God. I sat spellbound at the spiritual vista that was opening before me. It was so dazzlingly beautiful that my heart ached.

Were it not for Father Paul, there never would have been a Friendship House. It was he who encouraged me to keep going when the going was toughest. It was he who poured in thousands of dollars, through the years, into our work, factually supporting the first foundation in Canada for many months. It was Graymoor that, opening its doors wide to me and our Staff whenever the going was well-nigh impossible, soothed, healed, fed, consoled and strengthened us.

It was Father Paul, who almost a hundred years ahead of his time, showed me the principles and the ways of true Catholic Action. The things he spoke of are forever enshrined in my heart. Much of it will come into being many years hence, for his was a prophetic vision.[8]

Is not this an example of the words of a spiritual father becoming like a sacrament and absorbed into the heart as a way of life? Many of Catherine's own words would become such for others.

The Reverend Henry Carr, CSB

When Father Henry Carr first met Catherine, he was the Superior General of the Basilian Order in Toronto.[9] He had been instrumental in Catholic education: he taught at the university level for more than twenty years; he was superior at St. Basil's Seminary (1915–1925) and St. Thomas More College (1942–1949); he was founder and president of the Pontifical Institute of Medieval Studies at the University of Toronto (1929–1936); and he founded St. Mark's College at the University of British Columbia, and was superior there (1951–1961).[10]

Father Carr also took his spiritual life very seriously. Once elected superior general of the Basilian Order, "he devoted himself heart and soul to

8. Doherty, "Of This and That," 423.
9. McCorkell, *Henry Carr*, ix.
10. Shook, "Sermon Preached at Funeral Mass of Henry Carr," December 2, 1963.

the spiritual good of the community beginning with a renewal of his own prayer life."[11] Father Carr's method of giving spiritual direction was to stress the need for dependence on Divine Providence. "I thought it would be for the general good to let others catch the same idea of implicit trust in Divine Providence."[12] He also urged mental prayer upon his retreatants and directees while "leaving each soul to find its own way of talking and listening to God."[13] He encouraged the practice of ordinary penance as a link with the practice of the moral virtues. "If more mortification were needed, beyond the practice of the moral virtues, Divine Providence would provide it."[14]

Father Carr's spiritual direction "bears the hallmark of the great Carmelite, St. John of the Cross, who became his master during the years of his generalship, as he had been for some years before."[15] Apparently, Father Carr was profoundly influenced by the resurgence of Carmelite spirituality that occurred in the 1920s when the Church canonized St. Thérèse of Lisieux and proclaimed St. John of the Cross a Doctor of the Church.[16] He adopted St. John of the Cross's doctrine of the *via negativa* and stressed a supernatural knowledge of God over scientific theology:

> Father Carr held in high esteem knowledge of God by scientific theology, but he prized more the supernatural knowledge of God which is gained through prayer. Carr's preference for this direct knowledge of divine things, which he asserted again and again, did not imply a low opinion of knowing *about* God, which is scientific theology. On the contrary he thought it indispensable. His preference for the other kind of theology derived from his conviction that loving contact with God in prayer is the very foundation of holiness.[17]

Father Carr met Catherine in 1935 when she first began having difficulties with the Toronto clergy. She did not seem to enjoy the same degree of filial intimacy and confidence with Archbishop McGuigan as she had with Archbishop McNeil. "At this difficult point, when Catherine desperately needed someone whose opinions she could trust, Father Henry Carr,

11. McCorkell, *Henry Carr*, 93.

12. Ibid., 94.

13. Ibid., 95.

14. Ibid.

15. Ibid., 96.

16. Ibid.

17. Ibid., 97, 102.

the highly respected Superior General of the Basilian Fathers in Toronto, offered to help."[18]

Father Carr became Catherine's personal spiritual director at the same time he was appointed spiritual director for Friendship House in Toronto. Their spiritual direction was conducted almost entirely through letters because Catherine was in Ottawa much of the time working with the Friendship House there, and Father Carr was in Toronto. His letters to Catherine were formal in tone. He addressed Catherine as "Dear Baroness de Hueck," and Catherine addressed him as "Very Reverend," "Beloved Father," or simply "Dear Father Carr."

His formative influence on Catherine's development as a spiritual guide may be seen in the following ways, which also correspond with some themes of Catherine's spirituality in the Little Mandate: (1) His following of the spiritual doctrine of St. John of the Cross and his *via negativa*; and seeking God in the hidden depths of one's soul: "Take up your cross, My cross, and follow me. Be hidden." (2) His adherence to "the little way" of St. Thérèse of Lisieux: "Do little things exceedingly well for love of Me. Be childlike." (3) His insistence on trusting in divine providence for all things: "Sell all you possess. Give it directly, personally to the poor. Be simple, poor." (4) The practice of fraternal charity at all times: "Love, love, love, never counting the cost." (5) His preference for knowledge of God gained through prayer, rather than through books: "Fold the wings of the intellect." (6) His emphasis on using supernatural means to bring about social changes in the world: "Preach the Gospel with your life—without compromise!" (7) He taught Catherine how to conduct herself as a superior and how to accept human nature as it is, rather than what she would like it to be: "Be a light to your neighbor's feet"; "Go without fears into the depths of men's hearts. I shall be with you."

(margin note) Little Mandate

Passion for Justice

In one letter, Father Carr discussed the social doctrine embodied in the encyclical letter of Leo XIII, *Rerum Novarum*. The pope offered instruction on the ways and means within the natural order to correct the social evils present in the world. Father Carr emphasized that these were worthless without recourse to supernatural means because these social evils are always rooted in the fact that the world has turned away from God. Only

18. Duquin, *They Called Her the Baroness*, 143–44.

a return to God, a conversion of human hearts, could change the world.[19] Father Carr offered some very wise advice about not expecting the world to change all at once because of Leo XIII's letter.

Carr was aware that Catherine had witnessed "crying evils" in the social order and burned with zeal to right them. Her nature passionately desired to bring about change in the world, and she was impatient with delay. Father Carr suggested in this letter that she do what she could in the present moment and wait upon Divine Providence. The witness of her Gospel life would prove effective in the long term. Eventually, others would embrace her vision. Catherine benefited from Father Carr's emphasis on using supernatural means to change the world. From him she would learn to curb her impulsive, impatient nature while tending to the duty of the moment and to wait patiently upon God. This lesson she would eventually impart to her spiritual children at Madonna House.

In a letter filled with spiritual and practical wisdom, Father Carr instructed Catherine as to how those having authority over others should conduct themselves. First he offered his own experience as a religious superior. He stated that while the men under his charge were obligated to follow a rule of life pertaining to external conduct, at the same time, he was obliged to exhort them to advance in love of God, while respecting their freedom: "We must deal with human nature not as we would like it to be but as we find it. It is the odd, rare soul that hears the call of complete detachment of heart and close union with God here on earth. We must be satisfied with the rank and file, going along without much heroism. They need the sympathy of the man of God and the love, rather than harshness and fault-finding."[20]

In the above teaching, Father Carr applies his principle of using supernatural means to change the world: tirelessly encourage individuals to advance in holiness and leave the results to Divine Providence. However much Catherine was impatient to change the world, she was also impatient to root out her personal sins and defects, and eager to root out the obstacles to the love of God in others. Positively, she desired to see growth in holiness in herself and others, but kept encountering interior obstacles. Father Carr counseled that it was necessary to be gentle and patient with oneself and with others. Transformation and divinization are God's work, and these take time and the cooperation of a person's free will.

19. Father Carr, letter to Catherine, May 29, 1935.
20. Father Carr, letter to Catherine, February 13, 1936.

In addressing himself to Catherine's position as head of Friendship House, he wrote:

> When it comes to a lay person in charge of others, his position or her position as Superior is even less than this. I very much doubt if a lay person in such a position as a rule should preach to his or her fellow workers or in any way question their spirituality. He or she should do the work that comes along, at the same time anni-hilating himself and offering himself up as a victim to Our Blessed Lord. He can and should hope and pray, pray earnestly that God may lift up the others and draw them close to Him. He should not take upon himself to find fault with others touching their spiritual state. Even more than this, in the nature of things as we find them now, he cannot expect more than an odd one to see the things of this world and their relation to God in the same way as he sees them. He should leave this to those who have the spiritual care of the souls under him. I can only repeat what I have said above, that we must take the world and human nature as we find them, and not as we would like to see them.[21]

Father Carr discouraged Catherine, as a laywoman, from exercising spiritual direction with those under her charge, but he encouraged her to practice self-renunciation and offer herself as victim to Christ for the spiritual children entrusted to her care. This advice may have been culturally conditioned, owing to the unfamiliar role of the lay apostolate at this time in the Church. Or it could have been based on clericalism and an exaggerated sense of the religious life.

Nonetheless, this letter is a masterpiece of wisdom that served Catherine well as both the founder of the Friendship House and the future founder and spiritual mother of the Madonna House Apostolate. Through it, Father Carr taught Catherine a deeper respect for the sacred and inviolate nature of the internal forum of the human soul.

Spiritual Motherhood in the Marketplace

By 1935–36, Catherine's apostolate at Friendship House had brought her into contact with many people who were interested in joining her as members of the Third Order of Saint Francis and working in her apostolate to the poor. Young people began to approach her seeking help to discern a

21. Ibid.

vocation or for spiritual guidance in general. For example, in one letter Catherine expressed her concern for a young man who was engaged to be married within two months, but who questioned whether or not he should proceed with these plans, "because he might want to become a priest. This idea seems to obsess him and make things difficult for him."[22]

Here we see the beginnings of a pattern that emerged from this time forward: others began to see in Catherine a spiritual mother/*staritsa* to whom they could bring their spiritual problems for advice and discernment. In this case, the young man [Mr. B.] approached Catherine on his own initiative, seeking her assistance in his vocational crisis. Though Catherine wrote to Father Carr seeking his counsel and direction in the matter, which Catherine called "one of the most difficult questions of human life," she also felt more confident to offer advice on her own. In this letter, she informed Father Carr of her approach and asked for his opinion, as a spiritual disciple who was beginning the first fumbling efforts at helping others spiritually would ask the spiritual master to comment on his technique.

> With a prayer to the Holy Ghost, I advised him to do the following—and I hope that you will agree that I did right for I was very much worried. I suggested that he go into a retreat by himself and stay there for three days alone with the Lord, and then if he was still of the same feeling, spiritually and candidly explain that feeling to his fiancée, and at least postpone the wedding.
>
> Further I advised him to take the train to Toronto and go and see you, for he seems to have a wonderful faith in your judgment; and as I wrote to you before, is very much impressed and influenced by your philosophy and ideals. He agreed to do this, and I made arrangements for him to go to the Dominicans in this city for a three-day retreat.[23]

As already noted, 1936 began a time of great trial for Catherine as the storm clouds surrounding her apostolate at Friendship House began to gather. Naturally, she turned to Father Carr for guidance. As her previous letters to Father Paul Wattson, SA, testify, she continued to seek solace in the cross of Christ and experienced this time of rejection as a stripping, from which she would learn detachment. Catherine expressed a desire to see Father Carr and inquired of him as follows:

22. Catherine, letter to Father Carr, July 8, 1936.
23. Ibid.

Is it cowardly to want some comfort and encouragement? If it is, forgive me Father, for I am nothing really but a poor, weak woman, a great sinner—who as yet cannot fully understand that God himself has taken her at her word, where she, in the enthusiastic youth of her spiritual life exclaimed, "I love you. I want to be with you unto the end," and here it is the end or the new beginnings—Gethsemane or Calvary. I wish it were the latter, for then all would be consummated soon. But if it is the former, then facing me is Herod, the court of the priests, Pilate, the way of the cross. Father, I need you—you do understand, don't you? Will you see me? Please.[24]

This letter speaks for itself. Catherine was experiencing the harsh reality of rejection and the real possibility that Friendship House would close. A word concerning the closure of Friendship House reached her providentially on All Souls Day, 1936, as she faced the apparent "death" of her beloved apostolate. She alluded to the false accusations, the pain of rejection, especially by the clergy—"the court of the priests." One sees here Catherine's humanness but also her growing magnanimity, as she clung to the cross of the Lord and refused to defend herself publicly against her accusers.

Following this difficult period in her life, Catherine underwent a rigorous self-examination: "All I thought was love of God and my neighbor, all I did for inner and personal sanctification, suddenly seems false, untrue, and theatrically meant to impress others. Doubt enters my mind on the genuineness of all my ideas, actions, motives and intentions."[25] It would seem that God was purifying her motives and preparing her for the work that lay ahead—at Friendship House, Harlem, and later, Madonna House. She also experienced many temptations to despair and to abandon any further efforts in the lay apostolate.

The desire to flee from all endeavors for the Church and my spiritual self-betterment—visions of ordinary jobs and lukewarm Christianity call to me, seemingly saying, "even if you have not done it in full faith, you have done your share in awakening some to the dangers of today; let it be now. Leave it alone; you have every justification in doing so. Take from life what it offers best, of course without committing sin."

Only a very tiny voice seems to protest against this in my soul, whispering as it were, "indeed you have been but a poor servant,

24. Catherine, letter to Father Carr, October 26, 1936.
25. Catherine, letter to Father Carr, March 4, 1937.

but there is still time to become a better one. God has called you. You know it deep in your heart. His Grace [Archbishop] McNeil told you that plainly—God has called you to this hard, untraveled road of lay action. Keep on; do not shirk, even if you know that Calvary is the end."[26]

Discernment of Spirits

In the above letter, we are privileged to witness Catherine struggling to discern between two very different voices, that of the Holy Spirit and of the spirit of deception. Satan mingled the truth with lies and suggested that Catherine abandon everything for a more normal life. She had done some good, but now it was time for her to retire and "take from life what it offers without committing sin." This is a subtle and powerful temptation. The Holy Spirit speaks only the truth: she still has time to become a better servant of God. Father Carr reminded Catherine that her vocation was of divine origin. It had been confirmed by the father of her soul, Archbishop McNeil, and repeatedly reconfirmed by both Father Paul Wattson, SA, and Father Carr.

The greatest temptation, however, was to despair and temptations to commit suicide. In the following segment of the letter, Catherine expressed her feelings of total failure.

> Father, do not feel horrified that it comes to me. I am not giving in, but I wrestle with it as Jacob with the angel. Face to face, body to body, night after night, for it comes to me in the darkness. I know it is of Satan. He once came during my term of imprisonment by the Communists—it is suicide. I am, physically speaking, so tired of living. Since my marriage (1915) I have never had ONE year of peace or human happiness. I am an absolute failure, as a wife, a mother, a woman and now even as God's worker. I am weary and bruised and sick at heart. I am surrounded with enemies, and my loneliness is complete. My days are sort of a way of the cross inwardly and outwardly. There seems to be no hope, no future, no use to go on living—such are the whisperings of Satan. It is now two months after they began that I have the courage to write to you about it. But if I cannot tell *you* the truth, to whom can I?[27]

26. Ibid.
27. Ibid.

These temptations came at a critical juncture in Catherine's journey. She had the wisdom to recognize the necessity of bringing the whole truth of her interior trials and sufferings to her spiritual director, and her transparency of soul is evident. Even this was a humiliation. Catherine would later insist that a soul must reveal all to his spiritual director, hiding nothing. She learned in her spiritual direction the need for transparency if one is to discern the voice of God from that of the Evil One. Her experience with discernment in her own life later helped her as she guided others.

In a letter late in 1961, Catherine expressed to Father Carr her thoughts about him as a spiritual director, and assured him that she was praying for him during his recent illness. "God is merciful that He has spared you to us. Just having you in this part of the world is a blessing on all of us. I have never forgotten your kindness to me in the dark moments, the very dark moments of my apostolic life. And before it is too late, I really want to express that gratitude to you, Father, and tell you that you have been a great light in my life that has given me courage and a deeper understanding of my vocation. In fact, if it weren't for you, I don't think there would be a Madonna House. God preserve you for many years yet. We need you so much. May I say . . . lovingly yours?"[28]

Father Carr's reply was the last letter he wrote to Catherine: "It cheered and comforted me, and brought me back to those days in Toronto years ago. I have been following you closely ever since, almost as if I belonged to your band. You have always been in my prayers and that will continue until God takes me. I have always desired a visit to Combermere. It never seems to be possible."[29] Father Carr died on November 29, 1963. He never did make it to Combermere.

---

28. Catherine, letter to Father Carr, November 10, 1961.
29. Father Carr, letter to Catherine, November 16, 1961.

CHAPTER 3

Father Paul Hanly Furfey

Father Paul Hanly Furfey was a priest of the Archdiocese of Washington and the chairman of the Sociology Department at the Catholic University of America in Washington, DC. He wrote an article and a book that influenced Catherine very much: "Catholic Extremism" and *Fire on the Earth*. Their themes centered upon the need to apply the Gospel more radically to correcting social and racial injustices in society; and even more especially, he showed the relationship between liturgy and social action. For this reason, they appealed to Catherine's desire to live the Gospel without compromise. In this period before her arrival in Combermere, Father Furfey was undoubtedly the most influential spiritual director Catherine had. He remained her spiritual director from 1938 until she founded Madonna House in Combermere, Ontario, in 1947.[1] Thus, I devote a whole and extensive chapter to this principal relationship.

Catherine first met Father Furfey in 1937 in Washington, DC, when he asked Catherine to give a lecture for the Sociology Department at the Catholic University. In her early correspondence with him, Catherine focused on the new Friendship House she opened on February 14, 1938, in Harlem, New York, and all that was happening there—organization, staff, problems, etc. The reports about each staff worker were frequent, as Catherine was forming them in their duties and responsibilities, and only afterwards did she address her own personal spiritual issues. This reveals Catherine's priorities—charity first—the needs of others, herself last. This is

1. Duquin, *They Called Her the Baroness*, 155.

the most interesting and profound part of her letters: those parts in which Catherine opened her own soul to Father Furfey and revealed what God had been doing in her life.

During this period, more people were being attracted to the lay apostolate through Catherine's example and influence. Some who heard Catherine lecture on social or racial injustice were drawn by her words; others were attracted to what they perceived as Catherine's example of charity and holiness of life.[2] At this time, Catherine was frequently beginning to exercise the role of spiritual mother for the members of Friendship House. In addition, others, including priests, were seeking vocational or spiritual guidance.

As well as being Catherine's spiritual director, Father Furfey served as the chaplain to Friendship House in New York; consequently, he exerted a formative influence on its development. His letters responded to the issues Catherine raised about Friendship House staff workers and offered advice about how to guide them. Their letters reveal that Father Furfey took a great deal of care in forming Catherine. He supported her efforts to maintain a prayer life that was structured and consistent, and responded to her questions about the higher states of prayer. In the spiritual direction he gave to Catherine, one finds the theological principles that shaped both Friendship House and Madonna House, principles taught by previous popes, and that would be repeated many years later by the Second Vatican Council and John Paul II's *Christifideles Laici*—e.g., the dignity, mission, and vocation of the laity, grounded in the Sacrament of Baptism.

Father Furfey contributed much to the formation of this lay apostolate as it was lived at Friendship House and, later, Madonna House. "As Catherine's spiritual director he prayed much and was blessed with the gift of Counsel. His direction is clear, firm yet gentle and always presents her with a new challenge. He wants her to be a saint and constantly calls her to heroism. At the same time, he reassures her that her vocation is from God and thus heals her of the wounds inflicted by the Toronto experience."[3]

Catherine and Father Furfey agreed to begin with weekly letters, and Father Furfey stated that he would destroy all her personal letters as soon

2. Cf. the book of Catherine and Thomas Merton's correspondence for an example of her influence on Merton through her intense gospel way of life in Harlem. Wild, ed., *Compassionate Fire*.

3. Father Emile Briere, "How God Formed Catherine Doherty," 71.

as he had studied them.[4] This explains why there are fewer letters from Catherine to Father Furfey, and many more letters from him to her. Despite this agreement, Father Furfey saved some of Catherine's letters, which he later photocopied and sent to the Madonna House Archives at Catherine's personal request.

Some undated letters from Father Furfey to Catherine are masterpieces of spiritual direction. They deal with spiritual problems such as pride and discouragement, suffering, the necessity of taking proper care of the body, etc. These are called "miscellaneous" because there are no surviving responses from Catherine to these particular letters, Father Furfey having destroyed them per their agreement. Those letters that demonstrate his role as a spiritual father in forming his spiritual daughter, Catherine de Hueck, are of the greatest interest here.

During the period from 1938–1940, Catherine wrote to Father Furfey informing him that she was looking for a spiritual director "who would teach me to love God completely, absolutely, perfectly. But then I think often, can we poor mortals love like that at all?"[5]

Father Furfey responded by recognizing in Catherine's words a desire to be a saint, and he commended both this holy desire and her present spiritual path: "I think that the renunciation you are practicing, plus the works of mercy, plus, above all things, the liturgy, constitute the simple and natural way of progressing in holiness."[6] He then proceeded to outline the type of spiritual director that he thought Catherine needed.

> I hope you will be able to find a suitable director. It will not be altogether easy to do so even in such a large place as New York City. You need someone who is not only skilled in the direction of souls, but also who sympathizes with those ideals of the spiritual life which are represented, for example, by the Collegeville Benedictines and which mean so much to both you and me. Finally, your director would have to have the proper social viewpoint because your own intimate spiritual life is so inseparably bound up with the things you are doing in Harlem. This is, of course, perfectly natural and correct, yet I am afraid a great many excellent priests would fail to see the connection. I hope you will be able to find someone suitable. Let us pray for that end.[7]

4. Father Furfey, letter to Catherine, undated.

5. Catherine, letter to Father Furfey, March 31, 1938.

6. Father Furfey, letter to Catherine, November 15, 1938.

7. Catherine had encountered the Collegeville Benedictines when Dom Virgil

Catherine responded to his letter by asking him to be her spiritual director via mail. Father Furfey replied by offering Catherine his qualifications and deficiencies as a director, and what he expected of his directees, whom he referred to by the French term, *dirigé*—i.e., one who is led or guided by another. He assured her that he had an understanding of her apostolate and a good grasp of the principles of the spiritual life. Though he didn't demand obedience of his *dirigées*, he tried to "convince them by reason."[8] He also expected total honesty from his spiritual children, even concerning the smallest details of their temporal lives, and he advised Catherine that he hoped she would receive the Sacrament of Penance from him whenever possible.[9]

As their direction progressed, and Father Furfey came to know Catherine better, he began to move her away from the Ignatian approach to prayer, with its formal resolutions following each meditation to which she had become accustomed from earlier Jesuit spiritual directors, and towards a more Benedictine model—*ora et labora*—quiet prayer accompanied by apostolic activity.

> Now here comes the main point of my letter. As I read over your excellent and generous resolutions, it occurs to me that they are all in the Jesuit direction, whereas what you need is more emphasis in the Benedictine direction.
>
> Did anyone who knew you ever call you lazy? Of course not! You're the un-laziest person in the world. You're energetic to the n'th degree. And now when you get in the corner and go on retreat to extricate yourself, what is your solution? Characteristically enough, it is to whip yourself up to a still higher degree of energy.
>
> But perhaps that isn't quite fair. As I reread your letters I find that here and there you do remark that you need more tranquility. I do think you are on the right track there.
>
> Our Lord loves to have you rushing around hither and thither doing things for Him, but He also loves to have you relax now and then and be like Mary who sat beside His feet and listened to Him while Martha was so busy.[10]

Michel, the famous liturgist, came to Friendship House in Toronto to teach the members the Divine Office. She appreciated the Benedictine concept of *ora et labora*, which she later incorporated into the life of Madonna House.

8. Father Furfey to Catherine, no date.

9. Ibid.

10. Father Furfey, letter to Catherine, Good Friday, 1940.

Father Furfey outlined for Catherine his ideal standard of living for those who work among the poor. Catherine, deeply influenced by his views in her lay apostolate, implemented them at Friendship House and later at Madonna House. His advice would find a home in Catherine's heart as she developed both her thought about identification with the poor Christ in the marketplace of life and her efforts to heed the commands of the Little Mandate.

Father Furfey did not advocate "deliberate destitution," because "to live like that is a very special vocation exemplified by such people as St. Francis of Assisi and St. Benedict Joseph Labré. The normal standard of the perfect lay life is a means to keep all those things which are necessary for efficiency and to give up all those things which are not necessary for efficiency."[11] For all those who work among the poor and who seek to adopt the new social Catholicism which Father Furfey advocated,

> [o]ne should live on approximately the same standard as they. I deliberately say 'approximately' because it is seldom feasible to adopt actually the standard of the slums. The great advantage of this arrangement is that it gives rapport. As long as one lives on a different standard, one is not really of the poor. One is a stranger coming into their midst. Finally, we have the example of Our Lord and the saints. Christ lived in the slum section of Galilee and His life was indistinguishable economically from that of His neighbors.[12]

Father Furfey's letters are filled with practical advice. On the one hand, he recognized and affirmed God's call upon Catherine's life to be one of the "chosen few" and "rare" souls whose vocation was to suffer for the salvation of the world. On the other hand, he encouraged her to face her human limitations and to use natural as well as supernatural means to deal with the problem of discouragement: rest and prayer.[13]

ENTERING THE HEARTS OF PRIESTS

During the 1940s, people visited Friendship House and came to Catherine seeking advice and counsel in their spiritual and personal affairs. Among these were priests and nuns. During these years, we see an intensification

11. Father Furfey, letter to Catherine, January 22, 1940.

12. Ibid.

13. Father Furfey, letter to Catherine, March 6, 1940.

of Catherine's formation as a spiritual guide to souls, especially to priests. In her spiritual diaries, Catherine lamented to Jesus that she felt incompetent, unworthy, unprepared to give advice to anyone, especially to priests, because she was such a sinner herself and often felt like a hypocrite. She sought advice from her spiritual father as to how to proceed. In the letter that follows, we see Father Furfey preparing her for the work of spiritual direction. He reassured and encouraged Catherine in this new dimension of her vocation.

> Yes, I am perfectly sure that you are doing the right thing when you give your advice to priests and nuns. You must remember that there are some sensitive people who find it very hard to discuss their personal affairs with anyone. If one of these people comes to you and you were to refuse him the needed advice, he would feel terribly rebuffed and it would be just so much harder for him to turn to anyone else. Perhaps he might not turn to anybody else until it was too late to avoid a great deal of damage.
>
> So strike while the iron is hot. *Seize the opportunity when people come to you for advice.*
>
> Besides, you do have an expert knowledge of some things. Everybody does more or less have an expert knowledge of their own field. If the religious priest complains to you about the money-grabbing tendencies of his community, he comes to you as a person who has thought a lot about the problem of riches and poverty in the modern world. Why not advise him quite without hesitation?
>
> Yes, Catherine, you do have a gift of warm, human sympathy and understanding. You must give it freely to *people who ask you questions which you can answer.* When you don't know the answer, you always say so. On that basis you can't hurt anyone. You can benefit people enormously [emphasis added].[14]

Catherine's "exalted" perception of priests and nuns at first caused her to shrink from the idea of providing spiritual guidance for them. She regarded the spiritual life as their particular field of expertise. Nevertheless, she accepted Father Furfey's counsel in this delicate and important matter, and agreed to proceed, albeit with some trepidation, to embrace the path of spiritual motherhood that God was opening for her.

> I am glad that you so simply gave me the answer to a problem that has been worrying me for several years. I will follow your advice

14. Father Furfey, letter to Catherine, May 3, 1949.

in all the humility I can muster. I will walk softly and hold my breath, praying all the while not to be affected by the "revelations" that come my way. I know you are right; it was fear and a feeling of utter inadequacy, of helping such exalted people as priests and nuns, that predominated in me so strongly, because always the thought comes again and again, "who am I that I should advise advisors on spiritual life which is THEIR FIELD." But as you say, God has given me an added grace in the gift of sincere sympathy with people, so I must not misuse that grace but cooperate with it, trusting Him to uphold me in temptation.[15]

Catherine then described the visit of a young religious priest who was in a serious spiritual and moral crisis. Discouraged about the attitude of his superior and his most recent assignment, and with his vocation in jeopardy, he came to Catherine for spiritual assistance.

Last week was overshadowed with the visit of the priest, and the letter of the nun. The former affected me more than the latter, because his trouble is deeper. He, a brilliant young priest, has been deliberately put by his superiors into a position of a peg in a square hole, because he was encyclical-minded. Too much of that, in the estimation of his Superior, is bad for the revenues of the Order. The place he was sent to is a little, tiny provincial town, stagnating with the bourgeois spirit. He wilted and began drinking, got fat, hated himself, was nice to some women. They fell in love with him, told him so. He left them alone because of their marriage, not because of his vows. He concentrated on younger girls. Temptations came, were fought, partly succumbed to, fought again. He is attracted to young women. He is fed up. He wants to commit suicide or quit.[16]

Catherine then described her method of dealing with the priest, and its effectiveness. Her explanation reveals her developing gift of discernment and her perceptive understanding of human nature that is so essential in the work of the direction of souls. Note how she balances maternal tenderness with firm direction. The priest apparently found her guidance helpful, given that he expressed a desire to correspond with her.

With clenched teeth I sailed into him, *first gently, almost caressingly calling him back to Christ he once loved, then more sternly, then quietly* [emphasis added]. Then I wept from sheer exhaustion—(he thought it was for him); then I began over again. He promised

15. Catherine, letter to Father Furfey, May 4, 1940.

16. Ibid.

to go now at once to confession, to stick to the Order for three more years, to work and to reduce, cease drinking, leave women alone. Fine, but he wants to write. Letters like that are dynamite. Yet I agreed because he seems to so want to. He left full of thanks and some hope. I went into a panic, and wrote to you, because it rocked all my standards to their foundation.[17]

LEARNING THE ART OF SPIRITUAL MOTHERHOOD

In Catherine's letters that follow, we see an intensive growth in her role as a spiritual mother as people sought her out for this purpose. She was still at an early stage and repeatedly turned to Father Furfey for guidance and reassurance, especially when she directed the souls of priests. Father Furfey encouraged Catherine in her new apostolate to priests and others, and used the example of a French lay woman named Pauline Jaricot to increase Catherine's confidence that a lay woman could exercise this ministry.

Pauline Jaricot was a married lay woman in nineteenth-century France who desired to live a devout life. She was wealthy but embraced a life of poverty and lived with some lay female associates. She is considered the founder of the Society for the Propagation of the Faith.[18] "So she [Pauline Jaricot] faced the same problems that you face. Her example encourages me in my conviction that there is an enormously fertile field for lay women who wish to devote their lives to the service of God and neighbor without becoming nuns. Pauline Jaricot was very successful as an advisor of priests."[19]

Using the example of a nun in her novitiate year, Father Furfey told Catherine that she shouldn't expect too much from staff workers until they had been at Friendship House for one year. He reminded her that a nun was not given too much responsibility until she had been with the community for a long time. "So you mustn't expect your workers to learn the principles of your form of life at once. When your members have been there a full year, then they ought to *begin* to catch the spirit. In the meanwhile you are taking a very intelligent way of getting your people indoctrinated. You

17. Ibid.

18. Pourrat, *From Jansenism to Modern Times*, 475–77.

19. Father Furfey, letter to Catherine, May 1940.

teach your workers to think things through and to act from conviction not emotion. I think that's good training."[20]

A staff worker at Friendship House needed to leave because of her tense and nervous temperament. Father Furfey offered Catherine advice on how to do this in a way that would spare the person's feelings, given that it was the best decision for all concerned. He encouraged Catherine to help her come to this decision by herself, to see it as something good and necessary for herself. In this case, we see Father Furfey's exercise of the gift of Counsel and his sharing that with his *dirigiée*, while urging her to practice charity as the first law of spiritual direction.

> It would solve the problem nicely if she would decide on her own accord to leave. Perhaps you could help her to make that decision by telling her that you are afraid she is not getting what she wants in Harlem. I am sure that with diplomacy you can make her go home to Cleveland, yet feel that the decision was hers not yours. So you have to love her very much and really feel she should leave because it is better for her, not better for you. If you have that attitude you can send her away without bitterness.[21]

In the letter that follows, Catherine described the effect Father Furfey's counsel and direction had on her. "When I first read your letters I seem to absorb them vividly, as if my mental ears were deeply attuned to your words. They penetrate at once and then slowly as I reread them, they seep through and through me. And all the answers come easily and quickly."[22]

She was learning from Father Furfey the importance of leading souls to the love of God by exercising charity to the highest degree possible.

> Yes, that is just it. I must love her and others that especially irritate me, "much," like the Little Flower did the nun who irritated her. We always come back to that point no matter where we start from . . . to love. Here is the secret, the one and only secret of sanctity. You possess it in such a degree. Teach me, please do, how to love well in God and for Him. Always I stumble and fall by the wayside when it comes to loving truly and well in Christ. But I promise I will try. And when I mean try, I mean really so. I shall cleanse my heart from all irritation and start all over again. Pray for me.[23]

20. Ibid.

21. Ibid.

22. Catherine, letter to Father Furfey, May 6, 1940.

23. Ibid.

She once referred to Pauline Jaricot's last days which were spent in loneliness, persecution, and misunderstanding. Catherine had already had a taste of this and feared for the future. "I divined there a pain and a loneliness that is beyond human understanding, and I thought with fear and revulsion, that this too might be MY END."[24]

Nevertheless, Catherine agreed to reread Pauline's life to discover the similar positive points, and she especially enjoyed hearing that Pauline was successful in her ministry to priests. Catherine wrote of her growing confidence in directing priests, thanks to Father Furfey's direction: "I am advising priests, and I am doing it now with all the simplicity I can muster, and with peace and tranquility, because of your advice. You see, once the responsibility is not mine, once my spiritual director has spoken, there happens a very simple thing in my soul. It relaxes like a child in her mother's arms. It is so easy to obey, so very hard to command."[25]

Catherine was beginning to understand and accept herself as a spiritual mother and guide for others. In another letter, she referred to a correspondent, a priest, as her "*dirigé*" for the first time. She mailed Father Furfey a copy of the letter she sent to her directee for his approval.

> All in all it was a good strange day. For it also happened to be the day in which, obedient to your suggestion, I wrote the letter to my last "*dirigé*" and I enclose it for your perusal. Please tell me what you think of it and don't be too charitable. Just tell me if it is OK, or if I should have written otherwise. I simply wrote what was in my heart. You know the priest, I realize, even though I use his *nom-de-plume*, literally. I had a letter from him today and that is why I answered at once, and I am glad to say, without the slightest qualms of conscience.[26]

It would appear from this letter that Catherine was becoming more confident in her developing vocation as a spiritual mother. Because she was also growing in the knowledge and love of God, she could trust "what was in my heart" to be shared with her directee.

Father Furfey again affirmed Catherine's approach with her priest-*dirigé*. "You did a very good job. I think that priests often need feminine understanding and sympathy. He has been misled by the wrong kind of feminine sympathy. Now you are giving him the right kind. Another priest

24. Ibid.
25. Ibid.
26. Catherine, letter to Father Furfey, May 7, 1940.

could decide technical points of theology for him better than you. But *you* can give him something feminine which he really needs. And you *are* giving him just that."[27]

Following a spiritual retreat, Catherine shared the fruit of her prayer time with Father Furfey—which she was focusing on the exercise of charity. "To her [charity], I have dedicated all my efforts. I shall pray for the gift of true charity as I never prayed for anything. I see her breathless beauty now. Because of your words, my heart has been set on fire with hunger for her. I have no set plans except to practice it at once and always, toward all my fellow men. But I realize that she is more than that, and I will leave it to you and God through you to guide my faltering steps on that steep road."[28]

Father Furfey affirmed the primacy of charity in the spiritual life, and encouraged Catherine's deep natural capacity for its practice, while warning her about excessive bodily mortifications. His emphasis on charity served Catherine's vocation as spiritual mother both at Friendship House and later at Madonna House, which Catherine referred to repeatedly as a "house of love." Her work in both apostolates was primarily a practice of the corporal and some spiritual works of mercy. Father Furfey's spiritual direction was balanced and prudent.

> I am particularly glad that you emphasize charity more and more. That is the one big thing—the one thing on which we must never compromise. Poverty can be pushed too far, as you so clearly pointed out to me. Hard work can be pushed too far; overwork is bad. All the other virtues can be pushed too far. But who could ever be criticized for loving too much with the pure, unselfish love of charity? And it makes me happy that you are gifted with such a great natural capacity for love. Other people have to learn charity painfully and slowly; but you have merely to super-naturalize your enormous natural capacity. This, of course, is just a gift—not your own achievement—but what a precious gift. You don't need to be tense and worried about your work. All you have to do is to relax, let yourself go, and love God, your fellow-workers, the poor, and the ignorant, satisfied, complacent people who sometimes drift into your lectures.[29]

Taking up a new theme, bodily health, Father Furfey went on to relate one's spiritual life to one's whole social outlook.

27. Father Furfey, letter to Catherine, May 9, 1940.
28. Catherine, letter to Father Furfey, July 14, 1940.
29. Father Furfey, letter to Catherine, July 1940.

I have to trust you not to carry self-denial too far when health is concerned. If I am allowed to give you a direct order, please give your body the benefit of the doubt when you are uncertain and remember that one act of charity is worth a dozen merely physical mortifications. Also the charity is harder, at least it frequently is.[30]

Addressing the practice of humility, he encouraged Catherine to let her works of charity at Friendship House witness to the Gospel, while affirming the good work of others, especially the local pastors.

About humility—probably talk less about your work. The Vincentians have a rule (which they really seem to keep reasonably well) that they must not only not boast about themselves, but not about their community. Besides, your work in Harlem needs no advertising. Also try to develop enthusiasm for other people's work, not the work of people like yourself so much as about the work of people who are mentally a bit distant from you. Try, for example, to appreciate at full value the work of the priests of the parish and *point it out to others.*[31]

In many of the letters that followed Catherine spoke of the needs, problems and progress of the workers in her charge. Frequently, she sought Father Furfey's advice on how to manage and help them. She was developing a keen understanding of human nature, as well as that of the spiritual life, and this would grow as time went on.

In the next letter, we see Catherine's growing ability to assist the souls in her care with sound spiritual and natural remedies. We can see that she was not only applying Father Furfey's advice to herself—for example, regarding the care of the body in the spiritual life—but also to others as well:

N. went off the deep end in the matter of health. Her long holiday in New England brought her an acid stomach, the return of all her fears and inhibitions. She also saw her Jewish boyfriend, and the flesh reared its head up, which in her case, is quite a rearing. In my absence, no one diagnosed the case correctly, so she started losing weight, etc. With her, too, we had a nice talk, and she seems to feel better. Anyhow four pounds are back on her bones and the tummy is all OK now. Also we went over your retreat and decided to drop the Jewish boyfriend, for we had to choose between the two ways of life, Christ and the world. I admire her much; she has a stiff fight on her hands but she does not give up.

30. Ibid.
31. Ibid.

N. in the first enthusiasms of a neophyte, tried to be all things to all men, and do all that the "B" does, while I was away. Result: 5 pounds less in weight, and a lot of quirks. So I put him on a diet, took him off FH in the evenings and I am sending him for a 2 week holiday. The rest will settle itself when he rests.[32]

In another letter, Catherine continued to address the needs and progress of each staff member with Father Furfey, entrusting her care of them to her spiritual father. Catherine saw this approach as necessary on three points: (1) as part of her responsibility as the House Superior; (2) as part of her own practice of charity and duties of conscience; (3) as a spiritual direction "practicum" with Father Furfey in his offering of advice and criticism regarding her handling of various staff problems and issues.

Catherine was continuing to grow in confidence in her ability to lead and direct souls and in the recognition that feelings of unworthiness in this area were to be rejected. Her apostolate to souls was firmly grounded in what she called "Brother Routine"—all the spiritual activities that gave her strength and peace. She rightly discerned that this came from Another. In dealing with staff worker N, for example, Catherine recognized that somatic symptoms disguised and manifested deeper spiritual problems:

N. is still a problem that worries me. I am urging her to write to you, and then that will give you the opportunity to advise her; and she does need that advice badly. The sum total of her trouble is that she lives in a world where she herself is the most important item: she views all things from herself first. Oh, I am not saying that she is not generous, does not work hard. No. It is the result of her 'nerves'. Her past life, her physical condition. About that she worries to distraction. Personally, I think that all the tummy-aches are three-quarters imagination and concentration on self. But how to cure all that? I see only a thorough spiritual life and an anchoring of her thoughts in God, and shifting of point of interest.

However, before I REALLY begin that technique, I am going to have her undergo a complete physical check up. So next week will tell the full tale. What do you think?[33]

Recognizing her tendency to be severe at times, Catherine resolved to imitate Christ by concentrating on the practice of "tenderness" in her approach to staff:

32. Catherine, letter to Father Furfey, August 27, 1940.
33. Catherine, letter to Father Furfey, September 15, 1940.

So much for the staff. You see from my last three letters that they have begun to play quite a part in my weekly conscience survey. I am beginning to see, to develop a real spiritual technique to handle this whole situation. The thought came to me last week that one of the qualities of Our Lord was tenderness, and that it is not stressed enough in the spiritual life. So I have been writing my meditation on that virtue and have tried to apply it to them. It works. I confess that although through the last seven days I have appeared calm, collected, sympathetic, talking to all, listening in silence and answering quietly and being tender, inside myself I have been provoked, angry, impatient and worried in turn. The only progress has been in not showing it. Also, I have fought valiantly even if I say so myself, that old feeling of unworthiness to lead and direct them, that used to come over me, and has tried to catch me again. On the whole, though, I hope that I have brought some order out of chaos, given them a feeling that there is someone ready to uphold and settle them.[34]

Father Furfey affirmed Catherine's growing prudence in dealing with the souls of others: "A thousand congratulations on the success you are having with them. You have the warm human touch, which makes it easy to hold these sensitive high-strung people in line. I am glad, also, that you have so much sound common sense along with your exalted ideals. Your staff members are very safe in your hands."[35]

Catherine explained that her daily horarium brought peace and order to her life as spiritual mother of Friendship House, and helped her to concentrate on the practice of her favorite virtues in a Franciscan spirit:

I have caught up with my beloved Brother Routine, and feel happy and settled in his company. Mass, Prime, Compline, Way of the Cross, Rosary, Meditation and visits to the Blessed Sacrament follow each other with unfailing regularity, thanks be to God, and bring peace and tranquility into my life.

Uppermost in my mind are still my favorite virtues: love of God, poverty of spirit, full detachment, tenderness and knightly courtesy of St. Francis to all I come in contact with. I still persistently work on them under the general heading of the "Charity of Christ." Pray for me.[36]

34. Ibid.
35. Father Furfey, letter to Catherine, September 16, 1940.
36. Catherine, letter to Father Furfey, September 15, 1940.

During this period of intensive growth as a spiritual mother, Catherine continued with her progress reports on various staff members and outlined her own progress as a spiritual director. For the first time, she wrote of using the technique of speaking very warmly, gently, and tenderly, "like a mother to a four-year-old child."[37] These virtues of gentleness and tenderness were highly developed in Catherine, and she began to use them to nurture others spiritually. She found that this technique was highly effective in helping others to trust and open up to her.

> All through last week the same thought was present and it alone, CHARITY. Again I dwelt on the secondary, as it were, aspects of it. The humble handmaidens of Lady Charity—pity, tenderness, gentleness, politeness, kindness. And I began slowly to see a change of my own attitude to the poor. It is full of personal interest. I have shifted my point of attention from the efficient help of their material troubles to first making them feel good, pouring the oil of all the handmaidens on them. And it is really astounding what happens. They [her spiritual children] *open up as a flower to the sun, they beam and talk as they never talked before; they assure me when I cannot help them materially that I have done much for them,* etc. [emphasis added].[38]

IDENTIFICATION WITH THE POOR

There was also a growing awareness in Catherine of her suffering for others and her identification with their pain and troubles. Catherine was taking on the burden of her spiritual children, much as a mother might do for her children, a burden made lighter with God's help.

> *I suffer, as it were in them. Their sorrows and pains have become or are slowly becoming mine. I "feel" them acutely, whereas before I did not feel them so deeply within my OWN being. It is as if I was completely or at times partially one with them* [emphasis added]. The result is strange in my own self. I have the sensation of a very heavy weight on my shoulders bowing me down, and at the same time, of a Presence that lifts that weight off.[39]

---

37. Catherine, letter to Father Furfey, September 21, 1940.
38. Catherine, letter to Father Furfey, September 29, 1940.
39. Ibid.

We can also see Catherine attempting to live out the words of the Little Mandate: "Take up my cross (their cross) and follow Me, going to the poor, being poor, being one with them, one with Me." More and more Catherine was relying on, and experiencing, the Lord's promise in the Mandate: "Go without fears into the depths of men's hearts. I shall be with you":

> There is that *strong feeling of identification with the poor, and through it a strange and complete realization of what they undergo and what they must get from me* [emphasis added]. The words, "do unto others as you would have others do unto you," have sharply entered my consciousness, so that I DO KNOW what I must do for the poor that come to me. At the same time, the realization that this also makes me one with the Christ in them is strong, and strangely enough sweet, and not frightening as it would have been a year ago, though I confess frankly that it is slightly perturbing just the same. It lifts me up, out of myself, and at the same time, bows me down. Everything is clearer—my sinfulness, their needs and the Christ in them.[40]

In another letter, Catherine expresses realization and acceptance, for the first time, of the fact that she was, by God's will, the spiritual mother and founder of a new movement, a realization that prompted her to take action to improve her spiritual life.

> Friendship House has grown a great deal, physically and spiritually. Its members take it very seriously, and therefore they take me also very seriously. I am the Foundress, the top, the last word in many ways. Also, in their estimation, I am the model of what this as yet small, new venture of the Lay Apostolate of Catholic Action is, and into what it must grow.
>
> If I wish to or not, I have to face this state of affairs, and I, too, must grow up to my duties, obligations and desires of God, as it is He who shapes and directs us. I have failed in the past to understand this fact. I think that the reason for my failure is a sort of new realization of both God's will for me and His gifts to me. I did not realize that I am part and parcel of a new movement, small as yet, but which is bound to leave its impression on the sands of time, and on the history of the Catholic Church. Do I wish to or not, evidently God has placed on my weak shoulders the mantle of leadership, and now it is up to me to act accordingly.[41]

40. Ibid.

41. Catherine, letter to Father Furfey, November 1, 1940.

LIVING BETWEEN TWO MASSES

In order to "grow up" to her duties as spiritual mother and founder, Catherine made a firm commitment to devote more time to prayer, combined with an increase in bodily mortifications and sacrifices, and to give greater attention to the practice of patience and the building of Christian community.

> If this is so, then the answer is clear: I must do it. In order to do it well, I must throw myself more and more on God. The first thought therefore that comes to me is PRAYER, and ever more prayer, and especially the cultivation of God's presence through the day, by short ejaculations and lifting of my heart to Him. Also, if you agree, I shall take a full hour in the afternoon before the Blessed Sacrament; heretofore, it has been 30–45 minutes.
>
> Next to prayer I feel must come mortifications, physical ones, with your permission. (I thought of some that will not endanger my health.) And through Advent, I shall concentrate on the virtue of patience, not much I suppose, but for poor me very much. Say yes or no, please.
>
> A greater participation in the "family" life of the group, their recreations, parties, etc. which are the equivalent of the "recreation hours" of a community. I have held myself aloof in this matter. A greater exactness and promptitude in all matters pertaining to work and common affairs.[42]

She also spoke of the Mass as the source and center of her spiritual life: "Mass and Communion are still the wonder moments of the day, and the visits have become a necessity, the pause that refreshes, the break in a busy day, the moments of 'return' to the source of all strength. It is good to be with the Lord. My soul wants to cry out. Yes, Father, God has been good to me through the week."[43]

These practices became the foundation for her spiritual maternity both at Friendship House and Madonna House. One of her oft-repeated sayings was, "One can put up with anything by living between two Masses." She learned this phrase from the great liturgist Dom Virgil Michel.

42. Ibid.
43. Catherine, letter to Father Furfey, October 5, 1940.

A WORD FOR HER SPIRITUAL FATHER

In another letter, Catherine described what Father Furfey meant to her as a spiritual director. Her insights were the fruit of prayer and of a spiritual experience during Mass and Holy Communion. In this letter, Catherine wrote as a spiritual mother about what she desired for Father Furfey, her spiritual father: that he would assent to mounting the steep hill of Calvary. In this letter, Catherine was also beginning to share, for the first time, her insights concerning how the priest, as *alter Christus*, must be willing to share in the passion and cross of Christ as the price of drawing souls to the Lord.

> I begged Him to put your heart and soul on fire, to give you the same courage, boldness and thirst for souls that St. Paul your patron had. Let that thirst take the form of knowledge, books and studies, to know more and better how to set other souls on fire, only to bring others closer to you!'
>
> So I said to myself, and to Him, let his (your) class room be the crucible in which you, consuming yourself, spread far and wide these holy sparks of the Holy Ghost. And that like St. Paul, your spiritual countenance should be scarred with fatigue and lashed with effort, and weary with traveling for His sake. I begged Him also to make you see that you are by the very fact of your knowledge and writings the spiritual Father of the American Radical (from Radix—root—Christ) Catholic Lay Apostolate; that we, too, are outside your physical classrooms, but nevertheless your pupils and children who might benefit by this knowledge of yours. St. Paul, in weariness and exhaustion, traveled the small world of his day; you in modern comfort, but in the same utter weariness are called to travel in your field of action.[44]

Catherine expressed an idea that featured prominently in her spirituality—the Christian and the priest being "nailed to the other side of the cross." This was her way of describing how each disciple, but especially the priest, shares in the salvific mission of Christ. Her reference to the priest, spending himself and lifting people up "higher and higher," alluded to the priest acting *in persona Christi* in the Holy Sacrifice of the Mass. These ideas would be repeated as she continued to nurture priests with regard to their identity in future years.

---

44. Catherine, letter to Father Furfey, November 18, 1940.

I prayed because, like the Archbishop of Toronto, I now know that
the other side of the crucifix cannot remain empty, and that you
and I and all of us who try to love Him, must end there. And so
I tremblingly prayed that your charity might see this and mount
the steepness of Calvary. Poor dear friend and Father, was it well
and right that after you had spent yourself, and lifted all of us up,
higher, ever higher, and given us new life and joy in the service of
the Lord, I should repay you thus, by asking Him to nail you there
on the other side. And yet I think I asked for the right thing and I
think you will not be disappointed because I did.[45]

CATHERINE'S PRUDENCE

As the early 1940s progressed, Catherine continued to develop her gifts
for spiritual direction and demonstrated creativity and flexibility in dealing
with each staff worker at Friendship House according to his or her nature,
personality, and needs. In January, one of her most experienced staff workers was interested in leaving Friendship House, which caused Catherine
some concern. She began a process of discernment with the woman who
was attracted to the "Ladies of the Grail," a similar lay group working in
Chicago under the direction of a Dominican priest.[46]

Catherine's discernment of this vocational crisis was simple and direct: God had led this woman to Friendship House, and now she was attracted to "greener fields." She submitted her discernment to Father Furfey
for clarification and advice. In the following letter, she shared her insights
and observations about other Friendship House personnel and what she
had decided to do for each one.

Discernment of N's vocation: "N. has gotten the bug of the 'Grail Ladies' and is wrestling with it—today considering it a temptation, tomorrow,
the will of God. I am involved in this somehow. I guess she just wants to
have a listener to her 'talking aloud.' I know it helps. But as I see it, it is rather simple: God led her to us. Greener fields are not the distant ones. It takes
grit to stay. The whole thing perturbs me."[47] Other personnel problems:

> N. has lost 11 pounds, is getting medical attention for her meno-
> pause, is having her teeth fixed and is being organized to take

45. Ibid.
46. Catherine, letter to Father Furfey, February 22, 1941.
47. Ibid.

Father McSorley as a permanent confessor; and she needs one badly. On the whole it is a little easier, though all the above about her keeps me jumping.

N. is good and gives not much trouble. An adjustment will have to be made in his work. He desires to pray more. Here I will consult you after he has spoken to you about how much of that time for praying can be taken from the working time. Also, I am now in the process of rearranging his work and guiding him into the apostolate of men. There is much there that has been left undone for lack of a proper person to do it.

Miss M. worries me no end. She is not really fitted for this work, and I fervently wish that she find the convent she is fitted for. I have told you what I have done with her, so far so good, but it is still a palliative.[48]

Catherine recognized that the root of all these personality problems, aside from the obvious physical origins, was a lack of spirituality and mostly a lack of charity. "I am beginning to see why, in season and out of season you stress charity and again charity. It is the kernel of this whole business. Also, because of a lack of love, there is great subjectivism."[49]

Father Furfey approved of Catherine's management of her young staff workers and suggested that they were too introspective. The lay movement required great patience in dealing with "enthusiastic but somewhat confused young people who spend their time peering into the depths of their souls and talking about their insoluble problems."[50] Again, he stressed the need to practice charity above all else: "We just have to be infinitely patient with them, and kind and charitable and understanding. 'Where charity and love are, there God is.' We can't ever go wrong by being too kind and patient. 'Charity endureth all things.' Quite a program for us, isn't it? But if we can only live up to it, we'll get results."[51]

Priests and religious continued to approach Catherine for spiritual guidance, and she became increasingly more confident in dealing with them directly, although she always referred them to Father Furfey, and submitted her approach for his review and comment.

In one such case, Brother E., a member of a religious congregation in temporary vows, sought advice from Catherine about leaving his

48. Ibid.
49. Ibid.
50. Ibid.
51. Ibid.

community and joining Catherine's apostolate in Harlem. In his letter to Catherine, he told her of his personal reasons for wanting to leave the community; he generally opened his soul to her. He told Catherine that he had already written to his spiritual director, who offered his own advice. He did not want to be dispensed from his vows but from the community: "Poverty I should like to practice even more strictly and more literally than it is practiced in religious communities. Poor people in the world are shocked and scandalized at the ease and comfort in which clergy and religious of today live."[52] He asked Catherine to remember him in her prayers and gave her permission to write to his spiritual director. The evidence suggests that Brother E. may be the first religious to have been drawn to Catherine and her work.

In Catherine's reply to Brother E., she demonstrated great prudence. She offered her views and then referred him to those who were in charge of his soul.

> It can be a temptation of the devil against a true vocation; it can be passing shadows; it can be just physical tiredness or ill health. Into such details I am not privileged to go. For they are the domain of God, the soul, and those in charge of it on this earth of ours. I leave them to you.
>
> Personally I have no objections to your trying out Friendship House, if and when you finally decide to leave the Brothers. There are the 6 months of probation that will show us mutually if we are agreeable to each other, and if you are suitable to the work. So nothing is lost here. But before I go any further, I want to make quite clear a few points about the lay life of ours, so that you should be completely prepared, or at least as much as my poor words can make you.[53]

Catherine went on to describe life at Friendship House in considerable detail so that Brother E. would have a clearer vision of what he would be getting into if there were any doubts about his religious vocation. Catherine also referred Brother E. to Father Furfey, whom she described as "a great director of souls and a very holy and learned man. It will do you good in any case to get his view on the thing. Also he has known us since the very first day of our foundation and can enlighten you fully on any point of it that

---

52. Brother E., letter to Catherine, March 4, 1941.

53. Catherine, letter to Brother E., March 11, 1941.

might interest you."[54] Father Furfey and Catherine continued to collaborate together in discerning vocations and providing spiritual guidance.[55]

THE LIFE OF PRAYER: MARTHA OR MARY?

Father Furfey gave a retreat at Friendship House, and in his next letter to Catherine offered her spiritual direction on the contemplative aspect of being a lay apostle. He again encouraged Catherine to become more contemplative, an affirmation of what the Holy Spirit appeared to be working in her life at that time:

> What perverse trait is it in us that makes us look on Martha's work as important and on Mary's work as incidental? Yet we all do make that mistake constantly. We think we are doing God's will when we are "busy about many things." That's not the right way.
>
> The grace I wish for both of us after this retreat is the grace to realize that the way to get things done is to be contemplative. A very simple proposition which we all accept in theory readily enough; but why don't we practice it?[56]

Catherine reflected on Father Furfey's words in this letter. In her reply to him we see how she viewed him as a modern-day *staretz*, who was fulfilling the role of "doctor" and "counselor" in her life. Catherine understood and appreciated Father Furfey's words as an invitation to acquired contemplation, but she found them disturbing and frightening because they pointed to a deeper embrace of the cross and deeper death to self:

> Profound and vastly disturbing are your words: as a priest, when with that inner fire that God seems to give you so abundantly, you interpret His laws to us, urging, imploring, begging, beseeching us in His name and in the name of our eternal salvation, to love and serve Him ever better; and again, when you speak as a friend, a spiritual director and a teacher to me personally. It is as if with sure fingers of a spiritual physician or surgeon you probed the dark, turbid, sick spots of my soul and stirred unknown, or forgotten depths in them, leaving me aghast both at my neglect of them and at the strange possibilities in me. You frighten me and stir me, and urge and drive me, and bring new life to me; and yet I get sorely

54. Ibid.

55. Father Furfey, letter to Brother E., March 22, 1941.

56. Father Furfey, letter to Catherine, July 1941.

afraid and shrink from that touch, and fence and argue and defend myself against what I know to be the truth, because each new idea you bring out, each step you urge upon my restless soul, spell to me more pain.

Yet the things you speak about have a holy, fatal fascination for me. They are there—oh, how well I know that they are—but life has taught me that there is no birth without pain, that there is no creative effort without tears and sorrow.

You bid me to leave the newly acquired peace of an established routine, of a familiar, if steep path, and venture onto the lonely forbidding paths of contemplation. Not that of the mystics, but that of the thinker, to be sure; yet still face to face with God, and hence with pain and more pain. For the ideas will only take root and blossom in other people's hearts if and when I accept the precept that you laid down—to die to myself completely. And so I continue to wrestle with devil and angel. Pray for me.[57]

In her next letter, Catherine continued in a similar vein, reflecting on Father Furfey's invitation to become more contemplative and what this would mean in her spiritual life. She here affirms Father Furfey as a spiritual director and priest. For Catherine, he was someone who knew the nature of the interior life, not just from study, but also from experience.

Personally I am still afraid. Not as afraid as I used to be by the sheer majesty of God, but now by the intensity of what you are offering me. I seek, like the steel worker, the protection of the asbestos suit to approach the furnace where the metal melts. In this case, the protection of familiar things—distracting things, comprehensible, touchable things, with which I am familiar. Yet you bid me to leave them behind and sit at Christ's feet.

Yet, on the other hand, realizing all this, I also see that since you bid me to try, I will. To have you for a spiritual director means never to stand still, for the love of God urges you on, and so you urge the soul God has given to you. I do trust you completely; we all do. And what is more, we love you. To each of us you mean so much. Separately and collectively, you have our confidence *ad infinitum*.[58]

Catherine pleaded with Father Furfey to teach her the way of prayer so that she could teach it to others. She realized that she was venturing into

57. Catherine, letter to Father Furfey, July 14, 1941.
58. Catherine, letter to Father Furfey, July 20, 1941.

new spiritual territory and needed a father she could trust to show her the way:

> But since you bid me to start on a road that is so hard, since you want me to reorganize my life once more, then, Father, teach me how. I am like a child lost in the maze of the "do's" and the "don'ts." Take me by the hand and show me the way; and don't become intellectual on me either. Stoop down low to my littleness and teach me how to walk Mary's way from the first step. And when I fall and bruise myself, please be at hand to make it well, and start all over again. God bless you and don't forget to send on the first directions on that new road of contemplation.[59]

In subsequent letters Catherine continued to express her fear and resistance to contemplative prayer. She was always more comfortable with an active apostolate, as a "Martha." Father Furfey was offering her a new and challenging way to understand her vocation—"the idea of Friendship House" as he called it. Writing to Catherine about this "idea" behind Friendship House, he warned her about the "heresy" of activism.

> In moments of inspiration on the lecture platform you make young people see a very holy vision, a vision of what the Catholic life might mean in action. They thrill to that vision. It is the most precious thing you have to offer. It is this that makes them leave home and come to Friendship House; for Friendship House means to them the embodiment of that precious idea.
>
> Therefore, the success of F.H. depends principally on the vividness of that idea. If you allow the busy details of crowded Harlem days to tarnish the brightness of this idea, if this idea should ever become dim in your own mind, then F.H. would suffer a tragic loss.
>
> What a vulgar American heresy activism is! We say, "Let's get things done." That is good in itself; but how much less valid Martha's way was than Mary's. Won't we learn to sit at the Lord's feet and hear his words? If we do, then we become great, because those divine words are the most powerful thing on earth. They sweep all before them. They set men's feet on fire. Remember the disciples on the Emmaus road whose hearts were burning within them as they talked with Him on the way. So, if we become contemplative and gain deep insight, we can do anything. God gives His grace.[60]

59. Ibid.
60. Father Furfey, letter to Catherine, August 1941.

Furfey's words would profoundly influence Catherine's spirituality in the years ahead, as she often warned the Madonna House community against "the heresy of works."

A WORD ABOUT CONTEMPLATION

In the next two letters, Catherine and Father Furfey discussed the difference between "intellectual life" and "contemplation." She seemed to be confused by Father Furfey's synonymous use of these terms. To her mind, "intellectual life" implied the life of the mind, the work of the scholar, the thinker, etc. Perhaps Father Furfey's use of the word "idea" added to her confusion. She asked him to clarify the difference for her and wished to know where the various obstacles to the contemplative life originate.

> Now enters the fogginess and the haziness of my mind on the matter of contemplation versus intellectual life. As I said before, I do feel the urge and the need of the latter. I saw only too well its good results after the episode in Toronto—plenty of time to think, write, read and pray along with pain and suffering—it did the trick. But in that past as well as in the future, when I think of intellectual life, I neither did nor expected to enter into contemplation, for that is to me an entirely different story.
>
> Maybe it's because I have an erroneous idea of it. For me it's a separate entity from the intellectual. Oh, I agree that the latter is a living with, for and in God, who is the source of all good ideas in their clarity, but in a sort of a quiet, normal, peaceful way, a sort of turning one's face to His, a sort of laying out one's thoughts before Him. This I see and understand quite clearly. But contemplation— that, of course, is quite different to me. Somehow it means being always as if in church, and anyhow spending a lot of time there. It is a still listening in silence and a very concentrated silence at that—a groping in utter darkness, leaving all things behind, even intellect, and trying to learn how to love in a furnace of divine love that sears and burns our finite nature terrifically.
>
> So, summing it up, I see clearly my way to a renewed, intense intellectual life, lived in God, for God and through God in the simplicity of ordinary prayer and a certain amount of silent time to oneself; in recollection, reading and writings and meeting the right kind of people. But I don't see anything in this that has the remotest connection with what I understand by contemplation.
>
> I quite agree with you that the success of Friendship House is the idea behind it; perhaps I should say the ideas. I also agree

that nothing could be so calamitous to F.H. than the loss of such an idea.[61]

Catherine then quoted back to him the sentences about sitting at the Lord's feet and hearing his words, etc. She understood his words from personal experience: "That is simple, but is it contemplation? I don't know. I love to sit at His feet, but contemplation—no, I'm afraid of that."[62] She questioned where she would find the time for contemplation. She pleaded for his "advice and counsel" once again as something she needed more than ever.

Father Furfey's reply deals with each of the points Catherine raised. This letter offered a description of the two forms of contemplation. Again we see Father Furfey acting in the role of spiritual father and master, teaching Catherine the fine points of the spiritual life.

> About contemplation, first of all—we must distinguish between mystical or infused contemplation on the one hand and ordinary or acquired contemplation on the other. Infused contemplation is an extraordinary gift of God and there is nothing that we can do of our own efforts to acquire it. This seems to be the species of contemplation you have in mind for the most part of your letter.
>
> But there is another kind of contemplation, acquired contemplation, which is not a special gift of God except in the sense that any sort of prayer is a grace. Acquired contemplation means simply thinking about God or holy things in a particular way. What is this "particular way"? It is not discursive reasoning. It is rather a simple looking at the truth. If you go into church and simply think, "there is God; and here am I," and then you kneel there quietly with your mind fixed on the Divine Presence, not saying any prayer, not reasoning, but merely looking on God, with your consciousness occupied with the thought of the Divine Perfection—then that is acquired contemplation, and it is not above the capacities of any moderately serious Catholic.
>
> In my letter, perhaps I used the word somewhat broadly to include not only contemplation in the strict sense just defined but the whole mental attitude which accompanies it. A contemplative person habitually carries over into his life an attitude based on contemplation strictly so called.[63]

61. Catherine, letter to Father Furfey, August 21, 1941.

62. Ibid.

63. Father Furfey, letter to Catherine, October 7, 1941.

THE FRUIT OF CATHERINE'S PRAYER

Later, Catherine described her ideas as they emerged in prayer before the Blessed Sacrament. "I have embarked on the course suggested by you and confirmed by my little visits to the Blessed Sacrament. As I sit there in silence, things sort of clarify themselves. I just sit and look at God, and I guess He looks at me. And slowly, simply, ideas come into my head often with startling clarity, showing me how this can be settled and how that can he helped, and what to do next, etc."[64]

Catherine continued to discuss these "ideas" and how she applied them to the concrete circumstances of two of her spiritual children at Friendship House.

> I tackled N. and N. As yet I do not know the effect of that "tackling." I spent two and a half hours with one of them at the corner drug store over a soda, informal like, at the end of a very tiring and busy day. Then something in me was aroused and broke down the barriers and a great love and tenderness came into my soul toward her and toward all those who are perturbed and seek advice and light on how to love God more or live better. And I went home with a singing heart. Now why did I not know about that before?
>
> N. also was tired from all these lonely months at the helm. She has matured and grown up much since last August, and she needed cheering. Also, she was very, very tired. So I had her up for a whiskey and soda. The bottle had been here for four years gathering dust when it suddenly occurred to me that it could be used for the glory of God. With a little drink I cheered her up. I played cozy music on the radio. I got down to hard brass tacks there too, and showed her how brilliantly she had done the job during my absence, how much she had grown, how much I loved her. And then talked to her of the functions of FH as I see them now upon my return from a 9,000 miles trip.[65]

What is remarkable here is that Catherine was not the one-to-one spiritual director of these staff workers in the classical sense. She was acting as both a spiritual guide and a director of Friendship House, much like a novice-mistress who, in effect, did group spiritual direction, given the closeness and intensity of the community life. This approach served to nurture their spiritual lives in a very practical manner.

---

64. Catherine, letter to Father Furfey, December 27, 1941.

65. Ibid.

Next, Catherine unveiled another insight gained through contemplation—a developing vision of "a whole way of life" based on the hiddenness of Nazareth and an identification with the poor. This vision would grow and come to full fruition at Madonna House years later.

> The hidden/Nazareth aspect of the Lay Apostolate. I think much lately of Christ's hidden life. There is within it hidden somewhere deeply out of my sight a pattern for our Lay Apostolate. Again and again my thoughts come back to that strange unknown time of His. One thought especially fascinates me—identification with the poor. I am like a moth around a candle. Within that word "identification" I sense a whole way of life. At times I catch something of it and then the veil falls down again.
>
> One thing I know: he did not "help" the poor as FH helps. He helped by *being* poor in a sort of a different way from us. He did not take upon himself holy poverty. He WAS poor without taking it on. I flounder here, yet I know well that I must get at the bottom of that, for it is somehow tied up with that station of the Cross when He was undressed completely at death. There was also his near nakedness in life—in the stable, in the crib. I sense it will make a difference in my life. I want to imitate something there, strip myself more in some way, detach myself deeper somehow from what I know not yet, but I keep thinking of it. Have you any suggestions, any light to throw on my gropings?[66]

A GROWING HUNGER FOR GOD

By 1944 we see in Catherine a soul filled with longing for the living God. From Father Furfey, she sought guidance about how to grow in perfection and reported that she was also receiving numerous letters from people seeking spiritual guidance. "How to grow in grace and virtue, in wisdom and love of God. I see the steps to this—order, charity, justice, holy poverty, humility, and enveloping all of these is the mantle of ultimate perfect submission to God's will. Also within me grows the desire for a hidden life. More and more I want to be planted in the ground like a seed and die to myself. It is a desire, a movement, a need, a hunger, a fire."[67]

Catherine also informed Father Furfey that she received many letters every month, and most of these were from people who were searching for

66. Ibid.

67. Catherine, letter to Father Furfey, March 30, 1944.

help with "personal spiritual problems that are common to mankind and new only to the party involved."[68] She asked for advice on how to reply to these problems and suggested the possibility of writing a monthly newsletter containing general principles and remedies for them, as well as an exposition of the Catholic faith. In this way, she could respond to these needs and reach many people. In fact, at Madonna House, this approach would become one of the primary ways Catherine would communicate a word to her spiritual children—through newsletters and staff letters.

In one letter, Father Furfey offered an insight into who Catherine was in terms of her Friendship House vocation and what gave meaning to her life. He took seriously Catherine's passion to live the Gospel without compromise.

> Superficially your vocation consists in an enthusiasm for the Negro and a love of voluntary poverty. More basically, it is a belief that society can be helped only by a very vital and intense Catholicity. The thing that attracts people to you, the thing that gives life meaning to you, the thing that is most indubitably precious and wonderful about you, is precisely this conviction of yours—won through infinite travail—that *society can be reformed only by a shocking literal faithfulness to the truths of the Gospel, no matter how much this faithfulness may outrage human wisdom* [emphasis added]. Do you agree? If you don't, then we fail to understand each other, and we have to go back to the beginning and begin all over again. The principle which I just mentioned is then the touchstone by which you (and I) must judge all your acts and activities.[69]

In 1945, Catherine began to grow in the life of prayer. After practicing discursive meditation for many years, she developed "distaste" for this type of prayer. "Toward meditation I felt a great distaste. There was a strange desire, filled with an almost overpowering reluctance, for prayer, simple prayer, the one you call contemplation. During meditation I could not concentrate at all. I can usually concentrate on anything I want to concentrate on and that in the midst of bedlam. But now my attention wandered, and I got exactly nowhere."[70]

Being someone who was comfortable with the familiar, this experience of prayer confused and frightened Catherine: "With this clarity came

68. Ibid.

69. Father Furfey, letter to Catherine, April 4, 1944.

70. Catherine, letter to Father Furfey, July 25, 1945.

a fear: when meditations are distasteful to me, when all my old ways of prayers have become like old rags, when my feet were walking an unfamiliar terrain, could all this could only be an illusion, a temptation, to make me leave old familiar things? I was like a person lost, lost to all sense of direction."[71]

Catherine explained that this is why she wrote to Father Furfey in her letter of 16 March 1945. She was afraid that it "was but a mirage, such as I have seen in my childhood in the Sahara, put there by the devil to confuse my steps, make me go in the wrong direction."[72]

Catherine shared with Father Furfey that she had struggled to continue with "the old ways"—i.e., her old ways of prayer—and forced herself to meditate, but without success. "It is as if I and Christ and God the Father and God the Holy Spirit, but especially Christ, have reached a point where we have no need of words, like old married couples who understand each other without speaking. So do I and my Lord."[73]

She begged Father Furfey for spiritual guidance about these changes in her prayer life, and wanted reassurance and discernment that they were not temptations: "For things like that happen to saints or very good people and not to the likes of me. I am a great sinner, so why then this "understanding," this feeling that transcends feeling, that the time is past for words, that loving is sufficient, that He knows all my needs and will attend to them? That is all He wants me to do is to love Him."[74] It appears that Catherine was experiencing the prayer of simplicity,[75] with its illumination of intellect and will. She needed reassurances from Father Furfey that this growth in prayer was normal.

Guidance was necessary during this period because Catherine was engaged in spiritual direction more than before. She reported this to Father Furfey in the same letter:

> Then there is the almost uncontrollable desire for solitude, for that simple prayer, for conversations with God, to the exclusion

71. Ibid.

72. Ibid.

73. Ibid.

74. Ibid.

75. Royo-Marin and Aumann, *Theology of Christian Perfection*, 459–60. This prayer is also known as the "prayer of simple gaze," or the "prayer of simple regard," and it is characterized by a simple, loving, interior gaze upon God. The prayer of simplicity is regarded by spiritual theologians as the bridge between ascetical and mystical prayer.

of much of the action element in my life, and with this notice the change in accentuation that my life takes. In FH, I deal with souls more and more and less and less with the executive branch thereof. It seems to run itself well without me. It is the people in FH that strangely enough need me more. People confiding in me, sharing their joys and sorrows, asking advice. I have now 13 converts by mail. That has never happened before. Everyone seems to come here for doctoring of their minds, hearts and souls.

Are you beginning to see what I see? With the strange knowledge of everything falling into plan, the panorama unrolling clearly before my eyes, I seem to be able to—HELP ME GOD—to read human hearts. Father, I am afraid. I want to run away. Ten times out of nine I am right. I am mixed up. For one thing I know: if these are mystical phenomena, they are not for me. Please tell me where am I?[76]

Father Furfey's response was to inform Catherine that her experience in prayer was "just normal progress in the spiritual life."[77] It is unclear if Catherine understood her ability to "read human hearts" in the technical sense of *cardiognosis*, which is an extraordinary gift of God sometimes given to the spiritual father for the good of others.[78] Father Furfey did not comment on it in his reply, with which Catherine was not entirely satisfied. She gently chided Father Furfey in her subsequent letter for ignoring the fact that she was in great need of his priestly guidance, especially as she was now guiding others.

Most humanly, I do need you, although you are determined lately to ignore that fact. Yes, I need you because the road I am travelling is steep and still lonely; and there are many cross roads and precipices on it, and my eyes are not as strong as they once were; or maybe they have become wiser, and my steps not as sure as of yore, because perhaps my feet have been wounded sorely by the length of my travels. My will has been strengthened and my faith purified so as to lead those to where they want to go, and know where they should be going. I need your priestly hands to guide me. Remember that, Father. It is your primary office, taking precedence, it would seem to me, over books and lectures, which

76. Catherine, letter to Father Furfey, July 25, 1945.
77. Father Furfey, letter to Catherine, October 9, 1945.
78. Hausherr, *Spiritual Direction*, 32, 92.

would be sterile, were they not integrated into the living souls of men and women.[79]

Father Furfey's reply was to direct Catherine to train new staff workers to practice regularity in the spiritual life.

> I think regularity in the spiritual life is very important. It seems to me that there are exceptions to this rule. There are some people who seem to be able to live constantly in the presence of God, and it makes little difference if they pray at irregular hours—say, at different times every day. Perhaps you are like that. Be sure, then, that the schedule is adapted to the needs of the ordinary people whom you train, and not to the peculiarities of your own spiritual condition. Please train those young people in regularity.[80]

With this advice, Father Furfey recognized that Catherine's spiritual life was not "ordinary" but had gone beyond that of ordinary souls. For years Catherine practiced regularity in her own spiritual life: the careful following of a horarium. Father Furfey wanted to be sure that she remembered that these young people were not as experienced in the spiritual life as she, and would need to be trained to follow a regular pattern. This was wise, practical advice, quite typical of his approach to spiritual direction.

DETACHMENT FROM FRIENDSHIP HOUSE

During the next two years (1946–1948), another crisis began over Catherine's role and place in Friendship House, New York.[81] The outcome of this crisis resulted in Catherine's withdrawal from Friendship House and her move to Combermere, Ontario. Throughout this painful trial, Catherine received spiritual support from Father Furfey and abandoned herself to God's providence. Her spiritual insight at this time was summed up in the following letter: "I guess He wants me to detach myself from the very thing [Friendship House] He once asked me to create with His grace. So be it. His will is mine. And I am ready to lift my anchor once more, and set myself adrift on the sea of life. I am not as young as I once was, but with His help I

---

79. Catherine to Father Furfey, October 11, 1945.

80. Father Furfey to Catherine, November 12, 1945.

81. For full details about this crisis, its roots and causes, see Duquin, *They Called Her the Baroness,* 223–31.

shall serve Him the best I can wherever I go. Friendship House comes first, and if my absence from it will be for its best, I will absent myself. Amen."[82]

In the subsequent letters between Catherine and Father Furfey their discussion was not about matters of spiritual direction but concerning the ongoing conflict at Friendship House and how to resolve it amicably, along with other practical issues. Their correspondence continued in this vein through the summer of 1948. In some of her letters to him, she expressed her suffering at this second loss of her apostolate as a way of the cross.

> For now I am free. The last detachment is a thing of the past. Before God I am detached from FH, detached from the desire for, and every shadow of, authority and power, of motherhood, and all the rights of a foundress. I have to walk up the Holy Hill; I have to strip, finally and completely, and lay down on that Cross He had here for me from the dawn of days. Only then will my restless soul be at peace. Only then will the tumbleweed of God find a mooring place, to die to self so that FH may live, to die to self, so that God may live in me utterly, completely. That is the end of this journey inward that is the only answer that will make the lay apostolate secure and firm.[83]

These last letters show evidence of a deeper abandonment to Divine Providence and a willingness to forgive those who caused her to suffer and lose her place at Friendship House.[84] The following passage sums up Catherine's state of soul and demonstrates her humility, her trust in God, her willingness to forgive, and her determination to exercise that high degree of charity demanded by spiritual motherhood.

> It is a strange thing how the shadow of the cross follows me from birth till now, and I guess will follow me till death.
>
> We are all of good will. They are rare and wonderful people, and to me, in spite of the disagreements and misunderstandings, saints. Confidentially, because of this, my evaluation of them, I do feel that they are right in the final analysis. Namely, that I have been proven unworthy to head such a glorious movement as FH-USA. The Lord used me to lay the foundations, dig and mix its cement as a common laborer, the lowest type of laborer in the hierarchy of labor, and that is where I belong.[85]

82. Catherine, letter to Father Furfey, December 20, 1946.

83. Ibid.

84. Catherine, letter to Father Furfey, July 22, 1948.

85. Catherine, letter to Father Furfey, July 22, 1948.

Eddie Doherty called his biography of Catherine *Tumbleweed,* noting that "of her the Rev. Paul Hanly Furfey once said, 'She is God's Tumbleweed blowing through the world, wherever the breath of the Holy Ghost may send her.'"[86] In the following passage, Catherine's reference to herself as a "tumbleweed" indicates her willingness to allow the Spirit to lead her where He willed, in obedience to the Little Mandate, "Listen to the Spirit. He will lead you."

> A tumbleweed is a weed, and as such of no great use to anyone, except to be underfoot and to frighten horses. It is my true belief that without me they will do better, and this is neither pusillanimity nor false humility. This is my true and firm belief. I love them truly and sincerely and deeply, with a great love. I know they are sincere. If they really knew me a wee bit better they would really have something to complain about. So God in His goodness permits me to be a day laborer in His vineyard, and do the dirty work, and then gets real folks to do the more important and needed ones. And that is OK by me, for it is an infinite privilege beyond compare to even be a ditch-digger, or basement, or foundation digger for the Lord. Alleluia.[87]

Catherine's spiritual direction with Father Furfey appears to have ended in August, 1948. In her letters of that year she asked him to write to her occasionally, and their letters became more personal and social in tone. Although he was disappointed that Catherine was forced to leave her vocation at Friendship House, Father Furfey affirmed her new vocation at Madonna House. In one of his last letters, he wrote: "Things turned out magnificently, didn't they? Everything I hear about Combermere is good. Your works speak for themselves. God has blessed your work abundantly. That seems to me to constitute an unanswerable proof that your work is holy and blessed. May God continue to bless you! Be assured, I admire you. There can be no doubt on that point."[88]

On her part, Catherine expressed her gratitude to Father Furfey for his spiritual direction:

> I don't think you realize what you have meant in my life. You were one of my Spiritual Directors who really took me by the hand and,

86. Doherty, *Tumbleweed,* preface. Eddie Doherty was Catherine's second husband, whom she married in 1943 after her marriage to Boris de Hueck was annulled.

87. Ibid.

88. Father Furfey, letter to Catherine, May 19, 1974.

like St. John of the Cross, led me into the heart of God. My gratitude is beyond all telling, so is my love and my constant prayers for you. I don't talk too much about my feelings but I want you to know that I have loved you with a great love in the Lord since you took hold of my soul and shaped it according to God's will.[89]

Like Father Carr, Father Furfey never made it to Combermere, but much of his spirit of fatherhood remained in Catherine's heart.

---

89. Catherine, letter to Father Furfey, January 17, 1979. Note: Fr. Wild interviewed Fr. Furfey on June 2, 1988, at which time Father Furfey said she was "*the* pioneer of interracial justice." Personal communication to the author.

CHAPTER 4

Father John Callahan

Father John Callahan was a priest of the Diocese of Rochester, NY, and chaplain at Mercy High School. He hosted a weekly "Radio Rosary" in the diocese and visited Combermere for the first time in the summer of 1950. After hearing his series of talks on the Virgin Mary, Catherine was very favorably impressed, and the following year asked him to be her spiritual director. Their direction took place by means of letters until 1953 when Father Callahan came to Madonna House permanently to serve as the chaplain of the apostolate. There are also some letters from 1955, when Catherine was away giving lectures on racial justice and the lay apostolate.

During 1952–53, Catherine was moving toward greater spiritual maturity, and her letters to Father Callahan during this period reflected this. Often these letters contained spiritual poetry which was sometimes prophetic in nature and frequently referred to her relationship with Father Callahan or to her vocation as spiritual mother to priests. Father Callahan was the priest who directed Catherine through this more advanced stage of her interior life.[1] His spiritual direction was practical, concrete, and succinct. He was aware that, because Catherine was a founder and spiritual mother, he was guiding her as she, in turn, directed the souls of others who came to Madonna House, and as she directed the whole Madonna House Apostolate.

> His principal work amongst us was to be Catherine's spiritual director and thus take the responsibility before God of her

1. Briere, *Katia*, 129–30.

sanctification, which would mean, of course, the sanctification of the whole family. He asked of her every kind of detachment possible, total surrender to God's will, total trust and obedience to his direction. He was convinced that God wanted her to be a great saint and he directed her accordingly.

For instance, he gave her little or no praise. That was a terrible detachment for Catherine's passionate, outgoing and loving nature. Spiritually the benefits were extraordinary. He cut through her doubts, confusions and temptations in a masterly way and brought peace and assurance back to her heart. He was not only a good spiritual director for her, he was truly her father in the spirit and he led her with the assured hand of the master.[2]

Catherine had a wealth of experience to draw from in terms of her apostolic and spiritual life, in addition to her knowledge of human nature. The quality of her life up to this point—her consistent practice of charity—indicates a growth in union with God. Father Callahan guided and instructed her, but Catherine was already well on her way to becoming a spiritual guide in her own right.

THE DE MONTFORT CONSECRATION

Father Callahan had an intensely Marian spirituality; thus, he introduced Catherine and the Madonna House Apostolate to the Total Consecration to Jesus through Mary of Saint Louis de Montfort. On February 2, 1951, she and her husband, Eddie, made their consecration under Father Callahan's guidance.[3] Catherine attributed the "phenomenal" growth in her interior life and in her role as a spiritual mother at the Madonna House to the Marian consecration:

Madonna House was a new beginning, and yet it seemed no beginning at all—because no one believed but me that it was to be anything at all but a nice place for me and Eddie to live off our writings.

Then Mary's slavery—a growth overnight—phenomenal. Staff workers arrival. Growth in Summer School, of everything physical, inward, outward like roses in June. Then the change inward Father Cal wants me to write about, and of which I can say

2. Ibid.

3. Duquin, *They Called Her the Baroness*, 239. Catherine married Eddie Doherty, June 25, 1942, in Chicago.

so little. The discovery of a whole new horizon within myself. The life betwixt and between. Sights, sounds, gifts. Vows of poverty, obedience for life. Secrets of the heavenly King. A new life—and light, blinding, clear, on the apostolate, the truths of God; and love of Him and Mary that any minute seems to grow so big it must burn me up, annihilate me! But it never does, or did.[4]

These fragmentary phrases from her diary indicate the explosion of graces and insights that were coming to her then.

The Marian Consecration produced many other positive signs. First, it gave Madonna House its distinctive Marian spirit—hence the name of the apostolate, "Madonna House": "Madonna House is Our Lady's House, Her House of love: Her novitiate of Love."[5] Second, it led to Father Callahan's becoming Catherine's spiritual director and eventually chaplain of Madonna House. Third, more people began coming to Madonna House seeking spiritual guidance. Fourth, Catherine's interior life and spiritual maternity grew in intensity. Fifth, from Father Callahan's perspective, Our Lady herself began to form Catherine's spiritual motherhood through his direction.

Almost immediately, Catherine sought Father Callahan's advice about the life of prayer:

> Give me some pointers on inner recollection. How to go about it? There is a strange bend in me lately. My soul seems literally to pull me into silence. I cannot express how it comes about or the strangeness of that feeling, nor the urgency of it. It is as if the day were very hot, and all of me longed for the cool waters of the river, just to get into it and stay there, quietly cooling off. Thus my soul seems to desire urgently the cool rivers of God's presence. But the calls of duty, of work, of distractions are His too, and yet something tells me that somehow, in some fashion, the two can be reconciled. How I don't know.[6]

Catherine was growing in the life of recollection and described her experience of prayer, explained its effects, and why she discerned that this was genuine:

> Another thing bothers me. I almost hesitate to speak of it because I am such a Martha. Yet lately there has been in my prayers a

4. Doherty, *Spiritual Diary* No. 37, December 3, 1953, Madonna House Archives).
5. Father Callahan, "Confidential Notebook."
6. Catherine, letter to Father John, June 2, 1951.

strange change. The presence of God is almost palpable, at times overwhelming me with a shaft of great light, almost too strong to bear, leaving me sort of numb, and making me walk for a while afterwards as in a dream.

The only thing that assuages my fears and doubt is the sense of great peace, and growing desire to utterly live in Jesus through Mary. That surely cannot come from the devil.[7]

Catherine marveled at how many opposites and conflicting elements can exist concomitantly in one person's spiritual life.

It is impossibly strange, this spiritual life. In it so many things that should be strangers to one another come together—peace and shame, prayer, light and darkness, joy and gladness and such an overwhelming and constant sorrow for past sins and imperfections that continue and sharpen that sorrow without seemingly decreasing themselves. No wonder that God has given us guides to lead us along the way. One can so easily get lost and utterly discouraged.[8]

She also sought advice about her intense desire for poverty and detachment from created things:

I am as poor as can be. I do not know of any attachments I may have, but God must want me to examine myself again and again on this, since He seems to lead me along these lines when I pray before His face. On the other hand, it all seems of a piece—the new hunger or surge of desire for mortifications and of this stripping of myself, detaching myself more and more from all creatures and things.[9]

MARTHA MEETS MARY

Father Callahan offered Catherine sound advice about recollection and its relationship to action. This had been an issue in Catherine's spiritual direction for many years, and under Father Callahan's guidance it was finally resolved. His advice addressed each of Catherine's concerns, and his counsel was practical and succinct.

7. Ibid.
8. Ibid.
9. Ibid.

1. Recollection

> On recollection, it is like this to me. Recollection means the re-col-lecting, as it were, of all our forces and faculties, a calling-back of my mind, memory, imagination and will from all distractions and exterior concerns, to focus them completely on Almighty God, or the Guest in my soul. It ties in with what the writers call "the practice of the presence of God," and of course presumes a process of detachment from external affairs; a recollection of forces and faculties to withdraw into myself, and there adore and glorify and thank and talk to my Lord. Somehow it may be likened to a flame that is always burning, but if I place a blow-pipe behind it, it focuses into a point that will melt glass and iron. It is concentrated like a seraph's gaze, transfixed into one point, God and love of Him. So, I re-call, re-collect all my faculties to center them on Him alone.[10]

2. Reconciling recollection and action

   Father Callahan wrote that "we carry our cell with us, into which we can withdraw in silence and recollection whenever the opportunity presents itself; and which will grow with practice. Certainly silence and solitude are part and parcel of the spiritual life, and if we can't withdraw from the world entirely, we can periodically withdraw into ourselves, and be refreshed, like that cool dip into the fonts of our Savior."[11] Catherine later identified this interior condition of silence, detachment, and attentiveness to God as the "poustinia of the heart."

3. The change in Catherine's prayer

   He advised Catherine not to fight this palpability of God's presence but to "let it come. Sometimes God so rewards us and strengthens us to help us meet difficulties to come; if it is from the devil, he generally shows his hand by being too clever or going too far, and we are warned."[12]

4. Poverty and detachment

   Poverty is in fact good, but Jesus especially blessed poverty of spirit and the "non-demanding acceptance of our state. I still think the greatest detachment is from that of our own will."[13]

---

10. Father Callahan, letter to Catherine, June 9, 1951.

11. Ibid.

12. Father Callahan, letter to Catherine, June 9, 1951.

13. Ibid.

As Catherine's prayer life intensified, she was also naturally and painfully aware of the enormity of her sins. She described it for Father Callahan in this way:

> Suddenly, as if a curtain was rent, a fog lifted. I saw all my life pass before me with a clarity that was painful in the extreme, for it was as if a dazzling light shone on all my sins. I saw them in a true perspective, against Our Lord's Passion; saw the havoc they played with Him, the pain they inflicted on Him and the utter desolation they brought our Lady. When I say 'saw,' it was just that—nothing visionary, extraordinary, just saw a clear cut picture of it all with my mental or spiritual eyes.
>
> Now, nothing like that has ever happened to me in all my life. I was frightened too. The justice of God became a bit clearer and the weight of it too heavy for me to bear and the fear grew.[14]

Catherine experienced a moment of truth or "illumination" that signaled a point of deeper conversion:

> Then came a darkness the like of which I have not known in my life, and the devil became suddenly a reality. My soul hung for a split second on the brink of despair and I cried out, "Mary, Mary, help me," and it all vanished, and a great peace came. But with it came a resolution too, of going to confession, and then starting all over again once more.[15]

In 1952, Catherine described her view of the use of severity in spiritual direction to Father Callahan. Unfortunately, we do not have his response on this subject. Catherine thought that "severity" is useful in dealing with souls that are emotional, uncertain, vacillating, and pusillanimous:

> Modern men and women are so far removed from the spiritual that when they begin seriously to climb the ascent of truth there is need for severity tempered with charity. In fact, at times that severity *is* charity, but the art of the science of direction lies in knowing when to apply what and how. If I were a director, I would judge my penitents by the promptitude, the joyousness and the literalness of their obedience to my directions. But I also agree that the directors must examine their consciences constantly, because

---

14. Father Callahan, letter to Catherine, June 11, 1951.
15. Catherine, letter to Father Callahan, January 17, 1952.

when all is said and done, the direction of souls is bought at the price of the director's surrender to God.[16]

Catherine understood here that, although she was not a priest, she was called to exercise the role of being a spiritual mother to others. She was reading books on spiritual direction, which she recommended to Father Callahan—*The Three Ages of the Interior Life* by Father Reginald Garrigou-LaGrange, O.P., and *Spiritual Direction* by Pascal P. Parente. Perhaps this was a way for her to ground praxis with theory.[17] The former is a two-volume text that summarizes the content of courses Father Garrigou-LaGrange taught in ascetical-mystical theology at the Pontifical University of St. Thomas Aquinas (the Angelicum) in Rome. This work follows the teaching of three great doctors of the spiritual life—St. Thomas, St. John of the Cross, and St. Teresa of Avila. Its purpose is to provide a text of the principles of the spiritual life that can be applied to concrete situations.[18] The text by Father Parente offers "in one volume those scattered principles and rules of spiritual direction in order to give a more complete and systematic presentation of the subject, thus giving a much desired practical manual to both those who guide and those who are guided to salvation and perfection."[19]

FRUIT OF THE MARIAN CONSECRATION: DETACHMENT

The Montfort consecration implies the absolute giving of oneself to Jesus through Mary. "There is nothing whatsoever not included in this 'perfect Consecration.' We become 'divested' of everything, for our career, plans, possessions, spiritual goods—even glory—is freely 'made holy,' i.e., subject to the overriding will of Jesus. De Montfort insists that we pour out *ourselves* totally, completely."[20]

One may see this effort in Catherine to surrender herself totally to God through Mary by her attempts to strip herself of all created things, even her own will. To this end, she prepared to take a private vow of poverty

16. Catherine, letter to Father Callahan, January 19, 1952.

17. Ibid.

18. Garrigou-LaGrange, *The Three Ages of the Interior Life*, vol. 1.

19. Parente, *Spiritual Direction*, 7.

20. Fiores, *Jesus Living in Mary*, 210.

in light of her Marian Consecration, which she regarded as "the outward sign of my inward giving of myself in a special manner to Him Whom my heart has loved so long."[21] Catherine went on to explain more fully to Father Callahan what this private vow meant to her.

> I have asked His Mother this morning to take me into Her special novitiate and teach me there the full meaning of those deep simple words you wrote IN THOUGHT, IN WORD, IN DEED. There is so much hidden in them that as yet I know not, and that She alone can teach me.
>
> There is first detachment from all creatures, which means LOVING THEM IN GOD ONLY, and being ready to relinquish them, their presence, consolation, love and friendship always at His command. This leads me gently into a holy indifference that has nothing to do with a natural indifference that would be offensive to Him and hence to His creatures.
>
> It also means restricting oneself to the necessities of life. It means putting all my worldly affairs in good order.
>
> It means growth in trust and confidence in God and in His providence. Poor folks depend on others. I should depend in All THINGS NOW MORE THAN EVER ON GOD. It leads gently again to obedience, the apex of holy poverty: obedience to your directions; obedience to all other superiors, distant and proximate; an obedience to the most Holy Will of God as expressed by the duty of the moment, people, things and events of the day.[22]

The private vow of poverty was made on the Feast of the Purification of the Blessed Virgin Mary, February 2, 1952.

> MATER MEA
> PER MANUS TUAS
> With the consent and approval of my director,
> I, thy servant, humbly vow
> for a period of one year
> holy poverty
> in thought, in word, and deed
> for the honor and glory of God
> in the dear service of thy Son
> for the good of my soul.
> Catherine Doherty[23]

21. Catherine, letter to Father Callahan, January 26, 1952.
22. Ibid.
23. Doherty, *Private Vow of Poverty,* February 2, 1952.

The private vow of poverty increased Catherine's awareness that she was nothing before God and was dependent upon him for everything, a fundamental truth that Father Furfey had emphasized. In her direction of the Madonna House community, she encouraged this same spirit of detachment, consistent with the Montfort Consecration, which became a common devotion among its members.

In a letter following the Marian Consecration, she wrote of a growing detachment from the world and at the same time a great love for those who live in the world.

> It was like someone touched the eyes of my mind or soul and I SAW a thousand unrelated pieces of the spiritual life puzzle fall into place. It all connected. It all made sense. It all came together and it flooded my soul with an almost unbearable joy. It is as if the shadow of Christ Himself had fallen on me, like on the woman with the issue of blood, and what was dark yesterday became clear today.[24]

As Catherine detached herself from creatures she expressed a growing desire to *mother* others, to save God's children from their immersion in the world, and to bring them to a new birth in Christ through Mary: "My heart filled with such a detachment and indifference of the world as I had never experienced before. Yet, in that detachment was hidden, yet strongly felt, a great love for those who live by immersion in the world, followed by a burst of fire, *a zeal to get them out of it into Mary's arms, to be given over to Christ. My hunger for souls increased a hundred-fold*" [emphasis added][25]

Father Callahan confirmed that Catherine's detachment from creatures, her desire to practice charity, especially in the salvation of souls, and to mother others in Christ through Mary, was an indication that she was growing in sanctity. He wrote to assure her that what she described in her letter of February 8 was "the very work of the Holy Ghost."[26]

SPIRITUAL MOTHER OF MADONNA HOUSE

Evidence of Catherine's application of supernatural prudence to settle human problems in the Madonna House community is found in subsequent

24. Catherine, letter to Father Callahan, February 8, 1952.
25. Ibid.
26. Father Callahan, letter to Catherine, February 17, 1952.

letters. In this case, a young female staff worker and a male volunteer began an emotional relationship. The staff worker wanted to leave the Apostolate, but Catherine pointed out that she had made a promise for one year not to marry. In addition, the young people she was supposed to be forming depended on her being Christ-like in her relations with the opposite sex. Catherine encouraged her to use the one year to get to know the young man better and make a decision later. The staff worker agreed to this approach.

At the same time, another young man left the Apostolate after falling in love with another staff worker. She also began to see the need for promises of stability in the life of Madonna House: staff workers would commit themselves to this way of life for a certain length of time and so test their vocation.[27] In this context, Catherine asked for advice about this matter. Father Callahan affirmed Catherine's prudence in dealing with the first situation, and her intuition for the need of promises of stability.

"I think you handled it very masterfully, and gave exactly the right advice, or shall we say that continual prayers to the Holy Ghost really pay off in situations like that. But bingo, in the middle of it all, that promise not to marry for one year, which might be called a promise of STABILITY, has all the appearances of a saving grace, a spiritually-suggested solution. You use the term DEDICATION, which is correct, but that promise of stability looks like a foundation stone to build the dedication upon."[28]

The young man who left to marry was a convert, and Father Callahan wrote that converts required careful guidance because the new life of grace is still "tenuous" in them—"like the physical life in a baby, and needs a long building up on the graces that will come from Confirmation, frequent Confession, and the food of the soul, the Eucharist. Now, I don't deny the sufficiency of grace that the good Lord gives them; still it is best to hasten slowly with them. There are old habits to fight, and old sins to atone for, and grace and more grace is needed."[29]

In another letter Father Callahan referred a young woman to Catherine for the discernment of her vocation in life. The woman had been in a convent but left after a few weeks and returned to her former work in the world. She had received no support from her parents, and the work environment was not spiritually beneficial to her. Father Callahan wrote to Catherine to inform her that he had referred the woman to Catherine "for

27. Catherine, letter to Father Callahan, February 23, 1952.
28. Father Callahan, letter to Catherine, March 3, 1952.
29. Ibid.

the good of her soul. I place this in the hands of Mary and the Holy Ghost, and ask Them to use you as Their instrument in helping this soul make a decision about her future as to where she should go and what she should do."[30]

In asking this of Catherine, Father Callahan expressed his trust in her as a mother offers her children direction and guidance, especially in matters as important as a supernatural vocation. She thanked Father Callahan for referring this woman to her, and affirmed his reference to her as an instrument of Mary and the Holy Spirit as a "holy formula."[31] This "holy formula" would continue to develop under Father Callahan's guidance and prove highly effective in Catherine's direction of souls.

In another letter, Catherine reported to Father Callahan that this woman was seeking vocational guidance, Catherine again demonstrating her skill as a spiritual guide. Catherine perceived that the young woman was very tense, suffering from physical symptoms, and a variety of tensions over life, work, family, etc. Catherine saw "a spiritual lack of generosity. I say this in all charity—too much self-centeredness, the malady of our modern times, in which all is viewed from the narrow low point of self. I am constantly amazed at the powerfulness of the self-centered motive that reoccurs with such potent regularity in all the cases sent here. No wonder that the spiritual life is normal: it can conquer the self."[32] Catherine said the young lady could remain at Madonna House indefinitely, "that is, until the Holy Ghost has sort of quieted and settled her. He alone truly can."[33]

In her own spiritual life, Catherine shared her fears, temptations, doubts, which were put to rest by an act of absolute faith, and a remembrance that she was dedicated to Our Lady,

> the most generous of human beings and my full Mistress. Strange are the ways of God, strange and incomprehensible. Now it is stygian darkness, bottomless and frightening beyond seemingly all endurance. Now it is such a flood of light, love and joy, that also seems to be about to kill because of its sweetness. It all goes to show that indeed one must leave oneself in His hands, utterly,

---

30. Father Callahan, letter to Catherine, March 20, 1952.

31. Ibid.

32. Catherine, letter to Father Callahan, April 5, 1952.

33. Ibid.

completely, to be molded, picked up, thrown away, yet how exquisitely loving He always is.[34]

Catherine's experience of God's tenderness was teaching her to practice this kindness in dealing with others.

In an important letter to a troubled priest, Catherine told him that she was offering her prayers and penances for him. Here she revealed for the first time that her Apostolate was a "personal and hidden apostolate for priests who for a moment have known the darkness of Gethsemane but not seen the angel that came to minister to them; who like Christ, fell exhausted under the weight of the Cross and found the dust of the road soft and peaceful for the time being, even though it sapped them of the strength to arise and continue on to the Hill that was their destination on the day of their ordination."[35]

In these words, which reveal her spirituality of priests who, she believed, begin their ascent to Calvary on the day of their ordination, Catherine recognized that some priests experience the anxiety, loneliness, misunderstanding, and fear that our Lord did in Gethsemane. The "soft and peaceful" road, in this case, may be a temporary road, a resting place, a place of refuge or even healing. On a deeper level, this road may represent a path other than the one he was called to travel. It is a false path because it promises peace and an end to labor, but it does not lead to "the Hill" that the priest must ascend in order to share in the triumph of Christ. This "road" is, in truth, a detour that leads the priest away from his true vocation. This understanding of the priesthood shaped Catherine's exercise of spiritual maternity towards the many priests who visited her throughout the years, seeking spiritual guidance.

Evidently, the priest Catherine addressed in her letter had abandoned his priestly life, for Catherine wrote, "until in His Mercy God shows you the angel and lifts you up from the dust, the soft restful dust of the road, my prayers and penances will be yours. You probably never heard of me, and it doesn't matter much. All that matters is for you to know that there are in this world *many*, and I amongst them, who are willing to lay down their lives instantaneously, joyously, so that you may once more walk up the steps of the altar and say, *Introibo ad altare Dei*."[36]

---

34. Ibid.

35. Catherine, letter to an unnamed priest, December 20, 1952.

36. Ibid.

One aspect of Catherine's spiritual maternity to priests was to be the "ministering angel" who lifted them up from the soft, restful dust of the road, and helped them to continue their ascent to the altar, to Calvary; mystically and sacramentally in the Holy Sacrifice of the Mass; spiritually, through her daily prayer and acts of mortification and penance; and physically, through her daily activity sanctified by accomplishing the duty of the moment.

Catherine concluded this letter with an expression of love characteristic of her devotion to all priests: "This letter is dictated by an immense love, Father, for the whole priesthood, a love in the Sacred Heart of God. Accept it as such, and please pray for me." It also began, in earnest, her apostolate of "maternal victim-hood" for the souls of priests.

SPIRITUAL POETRY

The years 1952 and 1953 marked a turning point in Catherine's relationship with God. As she continued to experience the more advanced states of prayer, Catherine began writing spiritual poetry that described her relationship with Father Callahan as spiritual master to disciple, frequently with Jesus speaking in the first person:

No one will know that I wedded thee
with a slender gold band
that holds your hand in Mine.
No one will know but John My priest,
WHO IS MYSELF.
Remember that!!
And be obedient to his will.
IT IS MY OWN.
For it is time that you should know
that you are Mine,
and I want from you
utter surrender, perfect obedience, naked poverty,
and a heart filled with the passionate,
mad love of my cross and Me.
For who is Mine has for his marriage bed
at first the Cross.
This is My wish for thee, Catherina Mea,
whom this day I have clothed in the most

precious gifts taken from the hidden treasure
chest of My wounded Divine and Human heart.[37]

This poem speaks of a marriage between Catherine and Jesus—the reference to a "slender gold band" with which Catherine was "wedded" to Christ—although it is unclear if this is a reference to mystical marriage in the technical sense. She was to entrust the mystery of her interior life to Father Callahan "who is Myself," and she was to obey him as she would obey Christ Himself because Father Callahan's will is Christ's own. Only in this way would Catherine be safe. This is a constant theme in the mystical poems. Catherine's safety and security was to come through Father Callahan by means of perfect obedience to him. God was preparing Catherine, under Father Callahan's direction, to enter much more deeply into the mystery of the spiritual motherhood to priests.

In another poem entitled, *Refrain of Pain*, Jesus again speaks: Father Callahan would be able to protect her and would hold "the keys"—a biblical symbol for authority—to her questions.

> I am a jealous God
> and you are all my own.
> John knows that he is I
> to lead you.
> I charge him to guard thee well
> and teach thee the keys to
> what I want of thee –
> utter surrender.
> He knows the locks,
> he knows the keys,
> he knows the pain
> that goes into fitting lock and key.
> Tell him for me to be mercy-full
> by being mercy-less with thee,
> in leading thee to me
> with giant strides
> in the paths of love and pain,
> for I have need of thee
> to show the face of my Mother
> that your Russian heart will reflect so well
> when it is utterly crucified,
> like that land where you came from,
> and which she loves so well.

37. Doherty, "Crimson Red," 96–97.

Now rest upon my breast
Mary's Catherine,
and drift and drift
like a leaf in the wind
of my own love.[38]

Another feature in Catherine's spiritual poetry is certain prophecies, which would also shape her mothering of priests in later years. In one of these prophetic visions concerning priests in America, Catherine wrote to Father Callahan about a center of attack upon the priesthood by Satan. This word of prophecy was spoken in 1953 and has since become a reality in the United States—as exemplified in the exodus of priests in the second half of the twentieth and the sexual abuse scandals of the early twenty-first century.

> There is a restlessness among the young priests that is so tragi-cally dangerous. They, too, chafe under obedience. How the devil hates that virtue! Then there is such a cleavage between young and old priests! Both seem to dwell in a hell of their own making. I gathered quite a glimpse of it. And then that inner light that blot-ted all else moved and focused on these two scenes—home and priesthood. That is the plan of Lucifer. That is it. He is moving into the heart of nations—the family; but more than that, he is moving into the heart of the Church—the priesthood.[39]

This insight into the priesthood caused Catherine to experience and identify with "the pain of Christ," which she so assiduously sought to as-suage in others, and especially in his priests. This became another key fea-ture in her spirituality and in her exercise of spiritual motherhood: entering into the hearts of men and taking on their burdens and sufferings, and even sharing mystically in their wrestling with "all the powers of darkness." We will see in Chapter Five how Catherine's spiritual motherhood with priests was often influenced by an acute awareness of their sufferings and trials.

> Loneliness, intense pain, the sadness of Christ all continue un-abated. At times I seem to go into such depths of the pain and the sorrow and the sadness of Christ that I am, within myself, like one lying senseless where I fell. At other times it seems *I go into the depths of men's souls and wrestle there with all the powers of dark-ness at the bidding of God.* [Emphasis added]

38. Ibid., 310.

39. Catherine, letter to Father Callahan, February 6, 1953.

There is a strange pity, tenderness and such an upsurge of love (caritas) for all, that it shakes me to the very marrow of my bones, Father. I do know that my heart has been enlarged. Strangely enough again there is utter detachment from everyone and every-thing—again, an utter, loving surrender to Christ's will. Figure all this out. You alone can. I just go on floating on His will and yours, which is always HIS TO ME.[40]

CHILDLIKE OBEDIENCE

Catherine wrote to Father Callahan like a child in expressing her need for his guidance during this period. Staff members at Madonna House were reporting mystical phenomena associated with Catherine's presence, and this frightened her. One staff worker told Catherine that she smelled the scent of roses whenever she was near or when Catherine was praying for her. Catherine turned to Father Callahan for support and understanding. In the following letter, Catherine, longing for Father Callahan's presence, sent her guardian angel whom she named "Ivan," to obtain his blessing.

"Father John, I forgot the name of your angel, but I send Ivan to get your blessing. Oh, I need it so. Lord, Lord, Behold my hands raised in sim-plicity. I am only your strange child from a strange land your Mother loves. Foolish of heart, slow to understand. Father John is far. I am not confused, but a wee bit frightened in my natural self at all I heard. Yet your will be done in [me] always. Mother, Mother Mary, help me. Help me to stand still, still, still in utter surrender, utter obedience."[41]

The obedience Catherine offered to Father Callahan was grounded in the de Montfort Marian Consecration, with its concept of "holy slavery." For Saint Louis Marie de Montfort, this involved a "slavery of love and free choice, the kind chosen by one who consecrates himself to God through Mary, and this is the most perfect way for us human beings to give our-selves to God, our Creator."[42]

Since she and Father Callahan were both "slaves of Jesus through Mary," Catherine saw this act of obedience to her spiritual director as an-other way to offer herself totally to Jesus through Mary, another way to detach herself from her own will: "I am yours to shape, utterly it seems. I

40. Ibid.

41. Catherine, letter to Father Callahan, February 7, 1953.

42. Fiores, *Jesus Living in Mary*, 1163, 1157–67.

must admit to being tempted against this too. I did not like it at first, the word 'slave' in relation to you. But it came back and I don't mind it. In fact, I like it, as I think of it through Mary. We are both her 'slaves,' but naturally I am a lower slave than you, so it behooves me to be yours too. So you got love, trust, obedience, wrapped up in a loving slavery."[43]

Another theological aspect of Catherine's obedience was her keen understanding of Father Callahan's priestly power and authority as "another Christ." Christ was directing her soul through Father Callahan; therefore, she owed him the same obedience she owed to Christ.

"Out of this strange retreat has definitely come a clear, forceful awareness of *you*. It is as if God has put on you a klieg-light of immense power. My way to Him is quite clear—via His priest John (you), to His Mother, and then to Him. Such are the directions, the compass, of my way to Him, as if this whole retreat was just undertaken to pin-point this one concept. It deals with obedience, total surrender, and absolute dedication."[44]

Catherine admitted that such obedience was difficult for her, and she was tempted to reject it by another interior voice, which she identified as the devil: "'Utter nonsense. Why should you be a slave to a spiritual director? There is no need of carrying obedience that far. God is not asking that of you. You are crazy if you think He does.'"[45]

Catherine found divine assistance in the form of a light within her that rebuked the devil's lies: "Such a slavery is the essence of freedom, the freedom of the children of God. You must die to self through obedience. Obedience must be given to the visible Christ—a priest. Your priest, chosen by God and Mary for you, is Father John. Without him you are of no use to me. Offer yourself as a 'slave' to my priest John's will. Why? So that you, amongst many to come yet, will know that He is I.'"[46]

Catherine came to understand that God was preparing her for a spiritual motherhood that would involve "assuaging the inexpressible thirst of Love rejected." This became a constant theme in her writings. "That I have been selected (don't ask why—it is incomprehensible) from out of the world and called to the secret garden of inner solitude for the good pleasure

43. Catherine, letter to Father Callahan, February 14, 1953.

44. Catherine, letter to Father Callahan, February 17, 1953.

45. Ibid.

46. Ibid.

of God, and to assuage the inexpressible thirst of love rejected, so that in me God may know Himself and take His delight.""[47]

VICTIM SOUL FOR PRIESTS

Another aspect of her motherhood for priests was victimhood. This represents a high degree of love and sacrifice and a willingness to offer oneself "as a victim of expiation for the salvation of souls, or for any other supernatural motive."[48] The soul that offers itself as a victim "must be a soul that is well-schooled in suffering and has a veritable thirst for suffering. Under these conditions the director could permit a soul to make this act of offering itself as a victim and thus, if God accepts, be converted in its life into a faithful reproduction of the divine martyr of Calvary."[49] The evidence suggests that Catherine had practiced charity to a high degree for many years and was well schooled in suffering. She expressed the willingness to offer herself for priests in this letter to Father Callahan:

"I am beginning to get a glimpse of what the word "holocaust" implies. Pray for me, please, pray for me. At times it seems that I won't be able to carry on, to endure, to live this way. All of me craves rest, sleep, and I know that is danger, and the danger is close, close, close. I hold on to the names of Jesus and Mary, but it is the most dangerous danger that ever came here yet. Because I am alone in the sense that I am without you. It will be an all-out attack. I sense it. It is permitted for priestly souls. Oh, pray for me, pray for me. It will come soon like a tornado—pray for me."[50]

In his letters to Catherine, Father Callahan was succinct and prudent. He had received all her letters, and replied: "Continue as you have, in love, trust, obedience, and acceptance of His holy will. Do not look at your thoughts. This is important. Remember, for you, the state of life and its duties are to be your yardstick and criterion. Continue to write all as it comes to you. I shall read it and pray over it. So, be of good heart; continue, don't desire these things; receive them simply, report them faithfully; don't look at them, or dwell upon them."[51] ("Them" refers to extraordinary phenomena Catherine and staff workers described that she was experiencing.)

47. Ibid.

48. Royo-Marin and Aumann, *Theology of Christian Perfection*, 229.

49. Ibid., 230.

50. Catherine, letter to Father Callahan, July 8, 1953.

51. Ibid.

For example, Catherine described a "sweet taste in my mouth" that lasted through Mass and the Stations of the Cross and beyond, along with a pleasant fragrance that lingered around her; other members of the community also described such phenomena when in her presence. Catherine referred to this as "physical phenomena," but made no attempt to interpret their significance, if any.[52] She simply raised the issue with Father Callahan, who dissuaded her from giving them much attention. Father Callahan then quoted a long passage from Saint John of the Cross dealing with the need for the soul to relate everything to the spiritual director, and instructing the directee to turn away from any desire for extraordinary phenomena, since these do not imply merit of any kind. The rule of charity is supreme.[53]

During this period, Catherine continued to attract the attention of the sorrowful and the seeking. Following a lecture she gave at a nursing school, a woman approached Catherine and began to weep because she had lost her son in a plane crash, and she had lost her faith. She told Catherine "'I wanted to meet you. I knew I could feed on your faith. It shines like a light. I need you so desperately.'"[54] The encounter was significant in that it revealed again how ordinary people perceived Catherine as a spiritual mother: "I knew I could *feed on your faith*." [Emphasis added].

CATHERINE'S "FIAT"

Catherine's desire to offer herself to God for the salvation of souls, especially priests, became a frequent theme in her letters to Father Callahan. In one poem she wrote of being totally crucified, and her "fiat" to God was "complete."

> The night has come to stay.
> Where I abide there is no day.
> And yet I have a lamp, a light,
> that is darker than my dark night.
> Yet all the hidden ways,
> the heights, the depths, the endless plains
> stand all revealed through its dark light
> that shines so bright,
> and yet is darker than my night.

52. Ibid.
53. Father Callahan, letter to Catherine, July 9, 1953.
54. Catherine, letter to Father Callahan, November 9, 1953.

There is no comeliness in me.
I am a wounded thorn thing
that has been given over
to darkness and pain.
Fiat, Fiat, Fiat is my only refrain.[55]

In 1955, with her fiat complete, Catherine was ready to make one final sacrifice. On October, 30, 1955, with the consent of Father Callahan, she and Eddie took private vows of poverty, chastity, and obedience within their marriage.[56] This decision was motivated by the fact that the other members of the community were also vowing poverty, chastity, and obedience, and Catherine and Eddie knew that, as founder, she needed to set an example. Catherine did not expect the other members of the Apostolate to live in celibacy while she and Eddie enjoyed marital sexual relations. From this point on, Catherine and Eddie lived in separate quarters as brother and sister. It was a deepening journey into the depths of self-abnegation, poverty, and solitude that Catherine and Eddie were entering.

During this time, more priests came to Madonna House. In two of the last letters between Catherine and Father Callahan, she wrote of mothering priests and her mission to them: "I have a strange feeling. It is growing. *I feel I am feeding at my breasts, priests, men and women of the apostolate* [emphasis added]. How can I mother priests when they father me? I don't know, but I see the effects. I feel the mystery of it without knowing, and I am utterly at peace."[57]

A priest asked Catherine if he could rest on her shoulders because she brought Mary close to him. In this mysterious way, Catherine was a mother to priests: she nurtured them in their vocations, explained to them their true identity and the nature of their mission, and encouraged and loved them. She brought them to Mary, the Mother of priests. In this letter, she articulated that, and was amazed at this mystery.

With her fiat and interior crucifixion, Catherine's long period of formation had reached a certain spiritual maturity. She sensed that a new mission was opening for her—that of spiritually mothering priests.

There is in me a strange light. It is not mine. The "picture," the sensation, persists. A light, angels, archangels, powers, principalities,

55. Catherine, letter to Father Callahan, September 29, 1955.

56. Catherine and Eddie Doherty, "Private Vows of Poverty, Chastity and Obedience," October 30, 1955.

57. Catherine, letter to Father Callahan, October 10, 1955.

Our Lady, Christ, the Uncreated Trinity. I walk in the glory of the Lord. Our Lady is here, close, coming, and there is a light before her face; and in it a great role suddenly is given over to priests. Now the last work he has for me is PRIESTS. There is something I must do, for, through priests, and it deals with motherhood, and something elusive. 'Arise my beloved; winter is over in our land.'[58]

The time had come for Catherine to "arise" and exercise her mission to priests and others as spiritual mother. In the next chapter, we explore in greater depth this apostolate and Catherine's understanding and practice of it.

58. Catherine, letter to Father Callahan, October 10, 1955.

PART III

The Spirit Calls Catherine to Spiritual Motherhood

CHAPTER 5

Catherine's Spiritual Maternity toward Individual Priests

FATHER EUGENE "GENE" CULLINANE

Father Gene first met Catherine Doherty in 1934 while he was a seminarian in Toronto. In 1949, they renewed their earlier acquaintance; and the next spring, Catherine invited him to teach a summer school session in Combermere. He had studied under Father Furfey while doing doctoral work in sociology at the Catholic University of America. In August 1953, when Father Carr was his spiritual director, he wrote to Carr and told him of his intense attraction to Madonna House. He sensed the presence of God and Our Lady there in a way unlike any other he had experienced. He saw in Catherine a "greatness and holiness" he had never perceived before in the twenty years he had known her. He witnessed "miracles of grace," and many souls came to him seeking spiritual direction. He felt that God might be leading him to a Madonna House vocation. In 1956 he was released by his order to join the Madonna House Apostolate full time.[1]

Catherine's spiritual motherhood to Father Gene was not only for his own personal sanctification. Her "word" to him was also intended to build up the larger Madonna House community, and especially the other priests. The themes Catherine emphasized with him were priestly presence that rested on priestly identity, unity/*sobornost* among priests and laity, and an

1. Father Emile Briere, "Catherine and Father Eugene Cullinane."

increased awareness of the spiritual fatherhood of the priest and its proper exercise. In this way, Catherine fostered the growth of charity in Madonna House.

When Father Gene came to Madonna House, he became "nothing"—his superior, Father John Callahan, did not assign him to any post or position:

> For a man of his temperament, full of ideas, enthusiasms and nervous energy, this state of non-being purified him incredibly. Through this he learned not only humility and childlikeness at a deeper level, but also something about the power of the priesthood. One day, when he couldn't stand it anymore, he said to Catherine, "What contribution can I make to Madonna House?" And she answered, "Your presence, Father, your presence." This "word" became the deep foundation for the rest of his spiritual life, for the rest of his life on earth, 'Your presence, Father' [emphasis added].[2]

It is what the priest is—an "icon of Christ"—that is important, not what he does. Repeated often in her writings, she sought to reinforce among all priests clarity about their God-given identity. For this reason, Father Gene's presence was enough.

In a letter addressed to all priests, Catherine explained why the laity insist on calling priests "Father." She challenged priests to preach boldly the full Gospel, and exhorted them to do so with full awareness of their fatherly authority:

> Lately your voices have been muted. We do not hear them as clearly and as well as we need to. We need to indeed because the world around us is full of confusion and fears. Our pastures seem to be burning up.
>
> We [the laity] call you FATHER because you "begot" us in the *mysterium* of a tremendous love affair between you and God. Because you participate in the one priesthood of Jesus Christ.
>
> We call you FATHER, and we are your family, and we need you desperately. We need you where God has placed you, as He has placed a human father to wed a human mother and bring forth a particular group of children.
>
> We call you FATHER, and because we give you this awesome name, we somehow think that we are the ones who will fulfill your vocation, and who will fulfill your needs, for you have been

2. Ibid.

ordained for us, you have become our Spiritual Fathers, begotten us in the Lord and His Church.

Teach us how to love. Teach us how to pray. Inflame our hearts with a desire to wash the feet of our poor brethren, to feed them Love, and to preach to them the Gospel with our lives. Send us forth into the world everywhere, the world of poverty, hunger, misery, so that we may change it, because we heard your voice sending us there, the Shepherd's voice.[3]

Sobornost

In a talk to the priests of Madonna House, Catherine chided the priests for their lack of unity (*sobornost*) among themselves and with the larger community. She referred to compromises made with poverty and obedience, but saw something deeper than these external aspects of the Little Mandate's command about going to the poor and being one with them.

> The first poor are us. We are your first little children, your *anawim*. We need your guidance; we hunger for your direction; we hunger for a desire to be one with you. There is something in you that escapes this *Sobornost*. What is it? A sort of surrender. God is asking for EVERYTHING in Madonna House—a surrender of all of ourselves, with nothing left. It is in that realm, your dealings with God, that is your answer—the REALIZATION that they want to see the *icon of Christ* in you. It is nothing that you do, or don't do. *It is something that you ARE* [emphasis added].[4]

This word by Catherine was regarded as prophetic by Father Gene, and he responded with a meditation to help the other priests understand what Catherine was trying to nurture in them; or rather, what God was saying to them through their spiritual mother:

> What is Catherine really saying to us, Lord? What are you saying? Is it not that we priests have failed in some way to keep pace with the men and women of the Apostolate in implementing the Little Mandate in our lives? To really admit this in our hearts, Lord, requires fantastic humility and real humiliation. For we are your

3. Doherty, "An Open Letter to Priests."
4. Doherty, "Talk to Madonna House Priests," March 28, 1974.

priests, your specially chosen ones, and we are called by you to be
the shepherds, the leaders and the teachers of your little flock.[5]

Does not God desire a similar *sobornost* for all priests with each other
and with the people they serve? The average diocesan priest is indeed set
apart by God and consecrated for service to God's people. Sometimes he
has been set on a pedestal and has risked becoming isolated from the daily
lives of his people. In their seminary training, priests were traditionally
taught to be on their guard regarding excessive familiarity with the laity,
and to forge closer, more intimate relationships with their brother priests.

Catherine addressed this issue by saying that priests must work to
form unity/*sobornost* among themselves. This oneness already exists ontologically among the presbyterate within the sacrament of Holy Orders.
However, in practice, diocesan priests still may feel separate from one
another. Much depends on temperament, habit, age, etc., but Catherine
insisted that *sobornost* was essential for the priests regardless of these external differences, because *sobornost* among priests is founded upon faith
and charity.

Father Gene perceived a growth in unity among the priests and laity
of Madonna House, which he attributed to Catherine's spiritual motherhood—her love, prayers, fasting, and vigils for them and her spiritual director, Father John Callahan, and the exercise of his spiritual fatherhood:

> I see it [the growth in *sobornost*] as a glorious aspect of the great
> mystery that Madonna House is, the fruit of B's [Catherine] im-
> mense love for priests, of her prayers, fastings, and vigils for us.
> I know that it is the fruit of Father Cal's great love for priests, es-
> pecially for the MH priests, his steadfast loyalty to them and to
> the Apostolate through long years of waiting it out for the Lord
> in a strange desert and darkness that few of us, if any, know much
> about. Each MH priest has had his own crucifixion and thus
> shared with B and Father Cal, indeed with all of your priestly MH
> people, the reality that the holy cross we wear stands for.[6]

In several of Father Gene Cullinane's letters he revealed his thoughts
to Catherine about a number of personal issues and expressed gratitude
to her for her guidance. He reflected on his childhood memories of the
loss of his mother at the age of five, and his going away to boarding school
four hundred miles from home three years after her death. His search for

5. Father Cullinane, "A Meditation," March 31, 1974.
6. Father Cullinane, "Newsletter to the Madonna House Family," August 1, 1974.

a mother was realized in Catherine's spiritual maternity and in the heart of Mary within the Madonna House community.

In the following letter, he expressed his love for and confidence in Catherine's maternal love, which allowed him to open his heart to her and to share his pain. The letter is striking in its paternal tenderness.

> As the years go by I find it always more difficult to find any words to express my love for you. When I think of you and pray for you daily, and meet with you so beautifully from time to time in my dreams, it is as if, somehow, all emotions go to sleep, and we are together in the midst of an indescribable peace, deep understanding of one another, childlike joy and total trust. Nothing separates us, and there is no fear in me of anything that could ever separate us. I guess this adds up to a blessed and holy union of hearts that no words can ever describe. So, dear heart, we keep on walking together, hand in hand with Him and His Mother, into the Heart of the Holy Trinity.[7]

The importance of this letter lies in its summation of what Catherine nurtured in him through her spiritual motherhood—a deeper awareness of the spiritual fatherhood of the priest, and the emotional healing of his need for maternal and paternal love and guidance:

> A much deeper understanding of the gift of fatherhood came to me in the sacrament of Holy Orders. Your letter brought not only a deeper understanding of who I am as an MH priest, but also a real healing, for I have been crippled, at least emotionally, in this dimension of my priesthood, due to the fact that my mother died when I was five years old and my father, though a loving and holy man, was alcoholic, insecure and remote. In my formative years after my mother's death I was brought up by housekeepers and nuns.[8]

A particularly important example of how Catherine's spiritual maternity towards Father Gene was not only for himself but also for the other priests of Madonna House is that he was the first Madonna House priest to be stationed in a field house, Maryhouse in the Yukon. Catherine's letters to him in that capacity were the first of their kind and are fundamental to her understanding of what "your presence, Father" meant for Madonna House priests assigned to similar field houses.

---

7. Father Cullinane, letter to Catherine, December 24, 1979.
8. Father Cullinane, letter to Catherine, February 8, 1980.

FATHER EMILE MARIE BRIERE

Father Briere was originally a priest of the Diocese of Edmonton, Alberta, who celebrated his 60th anniversary of ordination in 2002. He met Catherine for the first time at Friendship House in Harlem in 1943 when he had been a priest for only three months. This was the beginning of a life-long relationship. He was one of the first four priests to join Madonna House as a full-time staff priest, and he enjoyed a close personal relationship with Catherine as a confidant and spiritual son.

Their correspondence began when he was in Edmonton, where he taught theology at St. Joseph's Seminary. During this time, he helped Catherine set up a Madonna House in Edmonton. He joined the Madonna House staff in October, 1955. Their correspondence reveals a relationship of tenderness, mutual respect, and great affection, with Father Briere frequently expressing a profound priestly love for Catherine and gratitude to God for all he had given to him through her. The following excerpt from an early letter reveals Father Briere's awareness that he is already a "child" of Catherine's maternal concern:

> You may still be quite alone, humanly speaking; who remembers a mother's great day, really? But your thousands of children—of which I am one—will, because of your love and understanding, spread that love far and wide, far beyond your wildest dreams.
>
> Because of what God has made you, because of what you had to suffer in the process, I love you beyond words because I love Him in you. His flame in your heart will shine and burn; His influence through you is just about to burst like a fire that has been quietly kindling for a long time and becomes a roaring tornado. 'Arise, my beloved, the winter is over . . .' His-Your love will conquer all. I mean it, and I love you, as a priest and a child.[9]

In her correspondence with Father Briere, Catherine touched on the themes of priestly loneliness, "spiritual nakedness," and the power of the priesthood to banish evil.

Priestly Loneliness and Nakedness

Priestly loneliness was the object of Catherine's attention throughout her life as a spiritual mother. Catherine understood the loneliness of the

---

9. Father Briere, letter to Catherine, October 12, 1953.

priesthood because she had suffered from loneliness for most of her adult life. She accepted her vocation to carry this cross with them. In the following spiritual poem, she described this aspect of her spiritual motherhood wherein Jesus is laying upon Catherine the loneliness of his priests. Noteworthy is the identification of priestly loneliness with Christ's loneliness— "I give you the loneliness of Myself." This loneliness is "wedded" to priests "when I make them Mine."

> I crown you (Catherine) as a queen is crowned by a king, with a crown of thorns. Lift up your hands, palms cupped for a gift. I give you the loneliness of all My priests, those who have locked their hearts, My heart, against Me, those My Father calls by My name. I give you the loneliness of Myself. No, child, not Gethsemani. The dark womb—Myself alone—the years of My life among men, the loneliness I wed to My priests as their brides when I make them Mine. I swam in an ocean of loneliness. This is but a small puddle. If you would follow Me.[10]

During Holy Week of 1960, Catherine wrote a meditation on Christ's loneliness and nakedness as she prayed for Father Briere and for all priests everywhere. During her prayer, Catherine described experiencing the presence of God: "All I know is that there was God, there was you, and the priests of the apostolate, and behind them, many, many other priests whose faces I could not see. And there was I."[11]

Catherine then began a meditation on Christ's loneliness, first as a child and youth, and then as a man—"a sea of loneliness" that would remain with him his entire life. In this loneliness, Christ was writing a "love letter to men."[12]

As Catherine continued she seemed to witness the stripping of Christ unto nakedness: "There are two kinds of the nakedness of Christ—the physical and the inner hidden one—for He wished it so. By His physical nakedness He atoned for all the sins of the body. Perhaps He allowed Himself to be without clothing to make us understand how holy the temple of our body is."[13] In the presence of Christ's nakedness we see our own reflected back to us as in a mirror, and we are appalled at the sight:

10. Doherty, "I Crown You," January 4, 1953.

11. Catherine, letter to Father Briere, April 15, 1960.

12. Ibid.

13. Ibid.

And for those who had eyes to see, Christ revealed the nakedness of His heart and His soul for us to look at, marvel, adore and imitate. So in His nakedness there is an inward mystery. Nakedness and loneliness seem to be one. For we are indeed always stripped in God's sight, but in our own sight, when we enter this loneliness, we behold our true nakedness; and most of the time we cannot stand the sight of it. And then, side by side, we behold Christ's inward nakedness. The comparison shakes us to the very depth. For we see what our naked soul and our naked mind looks like in comparison with His.

Ugliness against beauty, maybe? Weakness before strength. Sinfulness before infinite holiness. And like Adam and Eve we expel ourselves, covering our faces from a paradise that we have never known; the door of which, though, stands wide open for us to enter into.[14]

Christ was lonely "so that we might enter into His loneliness and abide with Him, and know that paradise begins here on earth."[15] Catherine is saying that to share in the loneliness of Christ is to taste, even now, the kingdom of God on this earth, because we are willing to share in his sufferings. The price of this joy, however,

was our entering into the raging stormy sea of Christ's loneliness, and walking toward the center of it, where He was standing. If this were to happen, then naked we would embrace a naked Christ and would become one with Him. And we would become immense in Him and be clothed in red garments, the color of blood, of pain and of love. For blood, pain and martyrdom would be as if they were not, and love alone would remain, the love we seek, the love we were created to find.[16]

This letter invites deep meditation and reflection. It is intended to present a spiritual challenge to all priests. They are invited to walk intimately with Christ—to be Christ in the world. Hence, they must enter the abyss of his loneliness and nakedness. They must embrace the cross of pain for the sake of love that comes with this loneliness. (Celibacy is perhaps the doorway to it.) They must also enter the nakedness of Christ and allow the Spirit to reveal themselves to themselves, and be purified. They are to stand naked before the Lord if he is to use them effectively. This is a frightening

14. Ibid.
15. Ibid.
16. Ibid.

quest, even for priests, and demands immense faith and trust in God. It demands, as Catherine suggested, walking on water, as Peter was asked to do, but not to falter as he did!

This "journey inward" that each priest must make is nothing less than an un-bloody martyrdom—the reference to "red garments" that leads the priest to imitate closely his Lord and Master in charity. The profound paradox is that this road of faith and trust leads the priest to discover the love he naturally and supernaturally seeks, the love he and all men were created to find. The price is high, but the fruits are priceless.

Should he, however, out of fear or selfishness, refuse to make this inward journey of faith and trust, he will find himself seeking love in places where it cannot be found. By doing so he runs the risk of accepting as genuine what is, in fact, a mere imitation—a "clinging to shadows, the substance of which was just the projection of childish desires."[17] These "childish desires" belong to the "old nature" described by St. Paul in his Letter to the Ephesians (Eph 4:22), that led him away from paradise—"down the slope of Tabor into the valley."[18] For Catherine, the loneliness of the priest was an integral element of his divine vocation to walk in the footsteps of Christ and to find his identification in Christ, especially in Gethsemani, where he was most alone.

In an open letter to priests, Catherine taught that "loneliness is a gift; it is God calling you to himself."[19] Her point is that all of us were made for God, and God alone can satisfy the human heart. Therefore, she saw loneliness as a way for God to draw us to himself: "I think that God created loneliness in us so that we might seek beyond our friends, husbands, wives, or communities, and enter into his real plan for us. It is by becoming one with the Trinity, which is the uncreated and first community, that we can become one with humanity."[20] Catherine appreciated the fact that priests, like all people, are social beings and need authentic friendships but never as a substitute for intimacy with God. She recognized the danger of seeking escapes from loneliness that would lead to occasions of sin or avoidance of God.

Catherine's word to priests about this universal experience of human loneliness is timeless. In the following passage, Catherine drew the image

---

17. Ibid.

18. Ibid.

19. Doherty, *Dear Father*, 46.

20. Ibid., 47.

of a "garden enclosed" from the Song of Songs as a "place" where the priest can be alone with God. She described the experience of intimacy with the divine in the Johannine image of the Beloved Disciple resting on the heart of Jesus where he could hear "the heartbeats of God." In this encounter of divine intimacy, the priest can bring his feelings of negativity and pain, and can find consolation.

> So when loneliness comes upon you, when you want to go and hide in some corner, when self-pity tosses you like a huge wave onto a beach full of stones, and you think you are going to be broken up by them, when this happens, close your eyes and repeat: 'In my heart there is a garden enclosed.' (Song 4:12) This enclosure is for God, and the waves have brought you into this garden where the feelings of self-pity and anger and all kinds of reactions will disappear. For if you go into that garden, you will hear the incredible sounds that seemingly only one man heard before, the heartbeats of God (John 13:25).[21]

Of her own "garden enclosed" she wrote beautifully: "But, lo, walk softly through the secret doors of my heart. No matter where my feet take me, no matter what task is in my hands, my soul is steeped in solitude; it is alone with God. Silence enfolds my heart and soul. Silence makes of them convent and cell where the Lord dwells."[22]

Catherine offered another antidote to priestly loneliness: "Do you know how to assuage your loneliness? Take the loneliness of another into your heart and immediately your loneliness disappears, or will."[23] Priests must love one another and love everybody. This love is an antidote to loneliness.

The Power of the Priesthood

In another letter to Father Briere, Catherine nurtured in him the image of Jesus Christ in his priesthood. Addressing Father Briere as a priest, she reminded him that he has power to destroy evil and to plant the seed of God in human souls: "Today I am setting you over nations, to tear up and knock down, to overthrow and to build and to plant. That is what you're here for, see? Because you destroy evil. You have the power to destroy evil, and you

21. Doherty, *Dear Father*, 46–47.
22. Doherty, *Lubov*, 44.
23. Doherty, *Dear Father*, 48.

have the power to plant the seeds of God in the soul of man. It's so powerful a gift that you have been given, and it's outside of yourself. It's not to a *man* named Emile; it's to a *priest* called Emile that it's been entrusted."[24]

Catherine reminded him that his priesthood was an immense light and a treasure of inestimable value—"a perfect gift" because it was an icon of Christ crucified, offered to the Father as a holy oblation:

> It's almost impossible to think about it—the immense light that you are in your priesthood. It's something that we, the laity, can offer up to the Father: Behold, here is your Son, deal with him gently. It's so immense, so great, that it's worth all the loneliness. It's worth everything. I am overwhelmed at the sight of who you are in your priesthood.
>
> "I believe, Lord, help my unbelief, because only your love could create a priest. I stand before it and I believe, but it's so stupendous that I cry out, Help my unbelief. It's so beautiful, *so perfect a gift.* Abba! *This is your Son.* Deal gently with him. Amen" [emphasis added].[25]

Catherine tells Father Briere that something will happen to him that will change him so he can adhere to Christ more deeply and identify himself completely with Christ, as if his heart becomes one with the heart of Jesus:

> I feel that something is going to happen to you that will make you enter into the kingdom of God in its depths. The kingdom of God is wide and large, and yet it's very small. You have to go through His heart. That's where it's wounded, you know. And when you do go through it you will know what it is that's going to happen to you. And you will be changed, in that you'll adhere to Him deeply; and you will find light in Him, deeply; and you will be His friend; and you will understand that the priest is a friend of Jesus Christ. But not only a friend. He's more than that. But this is a question of friendship and of a change of heart. And the Lord will see to it. He will blow upon your heart, and it will be changed. God the Father will say: 'Yes, this IS My Son,' and that means that you will be in the likeness of Christ so complete before you die that the Father will say, 'This is My Son.'[26]

---

24. Catherine, letter to Father Briere, August, 1980.

25. Ibid.

26. Ibid.

This was a powerful prophecy about who the priest is in God's sight, and another example of how Catherine challenged priests to become who they are by living lives of authenticity. If his heart is like Christ's, if he allows himself to be changed through the cross by embracing the loneliness, nakedness, and kenosis of Jesus, he will be so conformed to Christ's likeness that the Father will look upon him and say, "This *is* my Son."

That is what each priest is, in fact, ontologically and theologically. But it remains for the priest, in his sinful humanity, to take on the likeness of Christ in his life of prayer and sacrifice. This is the work of grace in him over the years of his priestly life as the Holy Spirit "blows upon" his heart and changes it.

In one letter of July 13, 1976, Father Briere expressed who Catherine was to him and spoke of the influence she had on his priesthood. The text provides clear evidence that Father Briere saw in Catherine a spiritual mother who carried God's presence within her, and for that reason he and other priests were drawn to her, as people were once drawn to the desert *ammas*.

In another place he referred to Madonna House as Catherine's "baby from God." He saw in her a spiritual mother who modeled the Christian virtues, especially forgiveness, tenderness, charity, and humility. Like the desert mothers, Catherine spoke a salvific and life-giving "word," full of mysterious divine power that answered questions hidden in Father Briere's heart and which bore fruit in his passionate desire to love God as she did.

Catherine shared "the gift of God" with him in a way that made God's love real for him: her "faith in the priesthood and in the Mystical Body of Christ shaped my spirit and influenced my life forever."[27] When Father Briere came to Madonna House, he said, Catherine's love "brought me new life." Catherine was a mid-wife that brought Christ to birth in him in a new and deeper way. He wrote,

> The greatest gift of all is God. You carry within yourself a special, holy and powerful presence of God and you have brought God constantly into my life. You share Him with all. Because *you carry Him*, His presence has come to stay at M. H. in a very special way.
>
> Because you allowed God to possess you, He has revealed Himself to me in a moving, beautiful and powerful way. Falling in love with Him, the deepest desire of my spirit has become a

---

27. Father Briere, letter to Catherine, July 13, 1976.

possibility and often a reality. *Because of your passionate love, I want to love God passionately.* God is your gift to us, to me.

Yes, that is your greatest gift, God, a gift so immense that it will take all eternity to praise God for His gift of you to me, and to thank you for your immense love. *You have led me into the very heart of God and never allowed me to run away!*

Your mercy has never failed me. My weaknesses and sins never trouble you very much except when they harm M. H. *your baby* from God. Then, of course, you are hurt and dismayed, but never angry.

Unfailingly, in every circumstance, half dead even, *you speak the word of God* and throw its light upon every situation. You reveal God as awesome, humble, wise, tender, infinitely loving and merciful, truly Father, Savior, Lover. You do so whether in ecstasy or in the nitty-gritty.

Your *word* cuts like a sword the evil in my heart. Your *word* heals and consoles as well. It is a two-edged sword. How often have you spoken simple and deep *words which answered questions in my heart I didn't even know were there* [emphasis added].[28]

FATHER SEAN[29]

In 1965, Catherine was corresponding with Father Sean, a diocesan priest serving in parish ministry and who was having trouble with his pastor. He wrote to Catherine seeking advice about this and his more general difficulties with obedience to Church authority. This correspondence reveals Catherine nurturing a priest who suffered from a common problem in parochial life: conflicts with authority, difficult assignments, and personality clashes with other priests, especially those with pastoral duties over him.

Father Sean's first letter, which speaks for itself, would likely resonate in the heart of many priests in similar circumstances: "My superior and I are absolute opposites. We have completely different outlooks on the needs of the parish and the apostolate. There is room for both of us in God's Vineyard, but I keep getting sour grapes! I can't preach what I feel God leads me to say; I can't give catechetical instructions, etc. This is a real cross for me. I can't believe this is what God wants. I can't believe it!"[30]

28 Father Briere, letter to Catherine, June 2, 1965.

29. A pseudonym.

30. Father Sean, letter to Catherine, June 1, 1965.

Catherine's response to Father Sean was grounded in her understanding of his priestly identity, his sharing in the saving mission of Christ. The priest must be conformed to Christ in all the stages of his earthly life, especially in his passion and crucifixion. In every way, she exhorted him and all priests to perceive their priestly lives from a supernatural point of view. Everything Catherine wrote to Father Sean must be understood in this light.

In her response, she first reminded him that God was molding him, as a priest, into the likeness of his Son. That molding is a progressively more painful process that eventually molds a man "to the Man of Sorrows and finally to the terrible face of the crucified. But a glorious, marvelous moment will come when, just by the touch of His thought, He changes our face into the radiant face of the resurrected Christ. It will happen if we have allowed His thought, His will and His fingers to mold us at His will and according to His love. I sometimes cry out because His molding fingers hurt."[31]

She told Father that he was sharing in the emotional agony of Jesus in the Garden of Gethsemani to console Christ and to be consoled by him. She exhorted him to find joy in this.

> For there was Gethsemani when the Son of Man was, according to psychiatrists, in a state of great anxiety and fear, as His humanity had to be, for He experienced all things human except sin. A neurotic anxiety, emotional darkness is part of our humanness, our humanity.
>
> So rejoice, at least let your soul and heart rejoice, and let that faith rejoice that has been such a cross and free gift of God to you and me and all of us, even though you are in an agony of spirit, mind and emotions. For being in Gethsemani means two things: It is to console the anguished Christ who had no one to console Him; and to be consoled by Christ in turn.[32]

Attempting to lift his vision from the purely human, Catherine told him that from a natural point of view there was no reason, humanly speaking, why he should obey his superiors. There was only one reason, and it follows from the imitation of Christ: "He was obedient unto death. So you are bound, unfree in every direction. Could it be that you are crucified? Hanging on a cross is the greatest protest that a man can make against

---

31. Catherine, letter to Father Sean, June 2, 1965.
32. Ibid.

another man. It is the greatest witness to truth, the best way to live with oneself."[33]

Addressing his concerns about "getting sour grapes" and not being able to do what he wants to do in the parish, Catherine offered him another way of looking at his situation. If he was willing to accept these difficulties as a sharing in the passion of Christ, God could use him in a more effective way.

> Let us remember that the first thing asked of us is 'to be' before God. Children to catechize, priestly duties to perform! True. All these are your duties as an ordained priest of God. But what if God wants you to be crucified so that something truly miraculous will happen to the children, so that your silence shouts loudly yet seemingly remains unheard but reaches the ends of the earth. What about that? What you need is the courage to strip yourself naked, become cruciform on a piece of wood and feel the bite of the nails. I shall storm heaven for you that you might see deep and see right.[34]

Difficult Assignments: Learning to Love

It seemed that God heard Catherine "storm heaven" for Father Sean. He was soon transferred to an even more difficult assignment, where the pastor had had six parochial assistants in six years, and five housekeepers! The pastor allowed no outside activities. This was Father Sean's third pastoral assignment in five years, and would be perhaps the most crucifying. He wrote to Catherine informing her that he was determined to submit to God's will and allow the Lord to do in him what he wished: "God, how I fear it! I was tempted to take off, but I prayed and willingly accepted the assignment."[35]

He also expressed a desire to be poor, and told Catherine that he had given away many of his material possessions: "I have depended on all these things for so long to fill the difficult hours and strain of following Christ. Now I feel that it MUST come to an end. I feel I must take all this time with Jesus. I feel I do not truly know Jesus."[36] His experience is a common one

33. Ibid.

34. Ibid.

35. Father Sean, letter to Catherine, June 10, 1965.

36. Ibid.

among priests, who are tempted to fill their lives with possessions and perks as a way to deal with the stress of personal trials and unreasonable pastors.

Catherine's advice was severe, demanding much faith on the part of the priest; yet she held out the promise of new life as well. She told him that this new assignment was a special grace for him—a way to learn love:

> Although this new assignment is emotionally shattering, and intellectually incomprehensible, spiritually it opens tremendous horizons. Why? It just could be because God loves you and He wants to teach you Love. Love is not liking. LOVE IS TO LOVE THE UNLOVABLE. LOVE IS AN AFFAIR OF THE WILL. LOVE IS CRUCIFIXION. Love has a twin in suffering. Suffering makes you Christ-like because it allows you to undergo the kenosis that every Christian must undergo if he is to empty himself of himself, as Christ did during His passion on the cross.
>
> God took you like Habakkuk was taken by the angel, by his hair, and He put you in His school of love, and He gave you the graces to pass the examination thereof. The rest, dear Father, is up to you. But I will pray for you daily.[37]

She affirmed his decision to give away his material possessions, and told him that this material poverty would prepare him for a deeper poverty—the poverty of giving up one's own will. Catherine understood from her own experience of dispossession the spiritual benefits of such a choice: "You ask for poverty. Now you are going to be poor, so poor that you can become intensely rich by possessing the fullness of Christ. It is good that you gave everything away. It is a good preparation for that poverty that God is going to ask of you, day in and day out, in that rectory. Yes, it is time that priests gave up trappings. I agree with you, but it is useless to give up trappings unless one gives up one's will too, the very essence of one's self."[38] Catherine assured him that she would pray and do penance for him because she was poorer than he, and that was all she had left to offer him.

In another letter, Catherine exhorted Father Sean to find strength in solitude and prayer, and to identify himself with the "anawim" of the Old Testament. For a man of Father Sean's large physical stature, intellectual capacity and assertiveness, this must have been itself a cross.

> The way to the knowledge of God, of the holy ones, is learned in today's silence of the heart, in the folding of the wings of the

37. Catherine, letter to Father Sean, June 15, 1965.
38. Ibid.

intellect, and in deep realization that one is one of the "anawim." Such a one is a poor man of the Old Testament who knows that he was a creature and therefore leaned on God and rejoiced in his poverty, and was strong with God's strength. He is also the poor man of the beatitudes; and he is the one "who knows" the Holy One because he knows who he is and he has taken the yoke of Christ and found it light because he never relied on his own strength but always on that of God.[39]

In the following letter, we see Catherine identifying with Father's pain and taking it upon herself in her continued efforts to "mother" Christ in him. Its importance here is in Catherine's description of her vocation as spiritual mother, which she was lavishing upon Father Sean. She compared her role as spiritual mother to him to that of Simon of Cyrene, who helped Jesus to carry his cross.

> You cannot leave me alone, for no matter how much you desire to, *I shall be with you. Your agony will be mine, your suffering will be mine, your doubts will be mine, and your joys will be mine, for God has given them to me, a privilege beyond compare. For this was I born of water and the Spirit, to share the pains of all humanity.* This I have been taught from my childhood by parents who loved God and understood that they had one duty in life, and that was to make their children love God, know God.
>
> They have given me that heritage of love and of knowledge, and have bid me to pray to the Holy Spirit to enlarge the vision that they have handed over to me. The vision is simple: *The pain of my brother is my pain. And since all humanity is my brother, then the pain of all humanity is mine.*
>
> Once in a while the Lord gives me a gift. A gift that surpasses all understanding: *The anguished heart, mind and soul of one brother or one sister. But when He gives me the heart of a priest, then though I tremble before this gift, I know He is calling me to Gethsemani to spend that hour with Him, or give of my love to Him, because the others slept.* So, dear Father, no matter if I hear from you or not, *I shall be with you in the humble task of Simon of Cyrene* [emphasis added].[40]

Catherine's spiritual motherhood towards Father Sean is also evidenced in her prayer for him. In one letter, she told him that she was praying that she would be "emptied" so God could love him [Father Sean] better

39. Catherine, letter to Father Sean, December 12, 1966.
40. Catherine, letter to Father Sean, December 21, 1966.

through her. One sees here that, as a genuine *staritsa*, Catherine practiced a self-forgetful charity on behalf of another, so he could grow spiritually: "Believe me, dearly beloved Father, you are a very important person in my life, for I love you intensely. I am afraid with a sort of love that few understand, because it isn't mine, it is God's. Desperately, joyfully, constantly, painfully, this love is forever beginning again. I try to empty myself so that he might fill me, so that he might love you better and better through my emptiness."[41] Catherine was not only exhorting him to practice kenosis, but modeling it for him in her prayers. In the same letter, she also taught him the simplicity of being a saint:

> Why is it that you cannot see, dear heart, that life is so simple, that all you have to do is let Christ run it? "My meat is to do my Father's will" no matter where it leads me. In the institution, out of the institution, in structures, out of structures, in prison, out of prison, in the ghetto, in the poustinia, there is only one law we have to obey. "And I say to you that men shall know you as my disciples because you love one another AS I HAVE LOVED YOU." The accent is on these terrible, awesome words, "as I have loved you." Put these words into the nitty-gritty days of an ordinary life and live them, and you will be a saint. Reject them, and you will make your own hell now and hereafter. For hell is a solitude that contemplates only itself, and can begin at any moment even as the kingdom of heaven begins here on earth. It all depends on our choice.[42]

Addressing his issues with Church authority, Catherine encouraged him to understand the Church as more than an institution. Her favorite model of the Church was the Mystical Body of Christ, and this view, for her, made all the difference. To the priest who thinks of the Church as merely an institution, Catherine says:

> Not once do you talk of the Church as the Mystical entity it is, the mystery it is. Always you talk of her as 'institutional.' I suggest you buy a pair of glasses, for you are awfully short-sighted. Yes, indeed you are. Why don't you meditate on this mystery of the Church that 2000 years of the shenanigans of popes, religious and VIP laity has not succeeded in destroying? Do you ever think of her as the Bride of Christ?[43]

---

41. Catherine, letter to Father Sean, July 18, 1969.
42. Ibid.
43. Ibid.

During the 1970s the Church in the U.S. suffered much theological conflict and confusion. Father Sean was in a large inner-city parish where he was drawn into the battle for civil rights and anti-Vietnam War forces. He knew Father Daniel Berrigan and others involved in these social issues. Father Sean got burned out and depressed, and phoned Catherine, who told him to visit Madonna House.

In these last two letters for our consideration, Catherine offered some insightful meditations to Father Sean on the meaning of the priesthood. These teachings were intended to build up a spiritual understanding of his priestly identity and dignity. Through Father Sean, one had a sense that she was also seeking to nurture this awareness in all priests. The points Catherine made in these letters are important examples of how Catherine used the Word of God in her exercise of spiritual maternity.

Priests may be great sinners, but they are saved sinners. Like anyone, priests can sin gravely, but they must have confidence in God's mercy. Catherine was trying to free Father Sean and all priests from despair by emphasizing the saving mission of Christ, which was also to them.

> Yes, I agree with you, it is quite possible you are one of the greatest sinners of all the priests you know, but you are always a saved sinner. But the word "saved," that's something fantastic. It is an explosive word, a word that shakes you to the very heart of your being, for it reminds us of Christ becoming a seed in a woman's womb, resting there for nine months and being born. It brings back that incredible fact that the Incarnation officially, humanly, began with the cry of a Child. And then there was his time as a carpenter, his Nazareth time. Then the urgency to go and preach, sowing the Good News to the four winds. And then the time of the Passion and death. All this is recapitulated in the word "saved."[44]

A priest is chosen by God. He endures struggle and surrender and struggle again to live the Gospel without compromise. Catherine, as spiritual mother to Father Sean, saw herself in the midst of his struggle, fighting with and for him.

> You are singled out by God. I know that He demands of you a totality of surrender, and you can't refuse Him. True, there is a struggle between you and Him and sometimes *I feel myself in the midst of it all* [emphasis added]. I wouldn't know how that happens. But the

---

44. Catherine, letter to Father Sean, November 12, 1970.

point is that the struggle always ends the same way: you surrender, but it doesn't mean you don't struggle again.

Yes, He is making a move. He has made many moves, and you have responded to each move. That is sort of a secret joy in my heart, and the clarity which you see in the Gospels is another joy. It scares you, but it doesn't scare me. That's exactly what I mean. Don't rationalize, don't discuss, don't theologize it away. DO IT. This has been the motto of my life. I have struggled, and God alone knows my struggle. And so I understand the struggle of others.[45]

Catherine understood her maternal vocation as walking with others, especially priests, into the darkness of faith, where God's light may be found. Like a mother leading her child, Catherine desired to "take by the hand every priest" seeking God, and nurture in him a deeper faith:

I don't know about the identity crisis (of priests), or the role crisis, but I know about the faith crisis. The identity is there, but I find people close their eyes and don't want to look into the mirror that will show them their identity. It's all tied up with faith. Who wants to go in that strange, terrible darkness that faith demands?

That's why I want to stand on the edge, between the darkness and the ordinary light. And I ask God to give me the courage to take by the hand every priest that is seeking Him and lead them into the darkness of faith which gets lighter as you go deeper into it. That's the question: to believe! Nobody can make the act for you, nobody! But perhaps someone can take you by the hand and gently say, "Let's go together."

I agree that the clergy is scared to death. So, Father, let's you and I pray; let's you and I take on their fears; let's you and I pray again and again and again that faith knocks at that door, until it opens. He said, "Greater miracles than I, you shall do." Let us believe that, Father. Come on! Let's begin! (emphasis added).[46]

Father Sean became a full-time Madonna House priest. In a recent roundtable discussion about Catherine's spirituality, he shared the story of his coming to Madonna House for the first time and the influence that Catherine had on his life as a priest.

Nothing about Madonna House attracted him on a natural level. However, he sat next to Catherine at the lunch table, and he *was* attracted to her. His lengthy written correspondence with her had been a source of

45. Ibid.
46. Ibid.

inner healing. From his description here, we can see that he had interior-ized much of what Catherine taught him. She was a spiritual mother to him so that he could be a spiritual father to others, so he could continue his particular incarnation in time as an icon of Christ. This continues in his priestly ministry at Madonna House.

> Once in while you find someone in your life who lives what he be-lieves. Catherine *was* what she believed. She had the most intense, ordinary, earthy and mystical understanding of the incarnation of any human being I have ever met. There was nothing that she couldn't squeeze back into the mystery of the incarnation. This was her starting point for everything: GOD BECAME MAN. Her Gospel clarity was intense: 'So, you want to love the poor, but you can't love your superior, your bishop, your pope, etc.'
>
> Do you realize what God has done? Catherine didn't go to the poor to teach them anything. We go to the poor to learn, and we cannot learn unless we understand how poor God is. There was something about this poverty that kept Catherine focused. She knew that the poor teach us how to love as God loves. This is why she wanted to spend her life with the poor. She believed that God was poor, and she just wanted to be with her Lover.
>
> When I ask, "Who am I?" I'm not asking a philosophical question under the guise of religion. Catherine isn't talking about either philosophy or religion, but IDENTITY: NOT WHAT SHALL I DO, BUT WHO AM I? Who am I in the Body of Christ? What happened to me ontologically when I was baptized? "Find Christ there in who you are." "If you discover who you are, you will discover what to do with the issues." This is the central issue: "Who am I?"[47]

---

47. Father Sean, *Catherine Doherty Roundtable*, June 1999.

CHAPTER 6

Spiritual Motherhood to Religious, Seminarians, and Laity

Although Catherine believed she had a special call of motherhood to priests, we have already seen that she was very soon drawn into the lives of the laity, the staff of Friendship House. As the years went on, people from all walks of life consulted her. In this chapter, we consider this widening of her charism as a *staritsa*. She became a spiritual mother to the whole church—seminarians, Religious, and the laity.

Her books to these groups took the literary form of letters from a loving, concerned mother to her children. *Dear Sister* (1953) was the third in this series of general letters—after *Dear Bishop* (1947) and *Dear Seminarian* (1950)—directing her spiritual motherhood to various states of life in the Church. She defined the main thrust of her letters to Sisters in this way: "In our correspondence we have spoken of many things, but our theme has always dealt, in one way or another, the Lay Apostolate of Catholic Action."[1]

In *Dear Seminarian*, Catherine offered wise and practical advice about the major issues pertaining to priestly identity and formation.[2] She instructed the seminarians that they must first practice what they will be called upon to teach to the people: "The first thing I want to speak about is

1. Doherty, *Dear Sister*, 66.
2. Doherty, *Dear Seminarian*, 6.

prayer. We the laity need to know how to pray. Will you learn, so that when the time comes you can teach us?"[3]

Catherine's spiritual motherhood among the laity was the first, and the most extensive, expression of her vocation as *staritsa*. "You need someone to teach you again the first principles of God's word. You need milk, not solid food" (Heb 5:12). In her thousands of letters to laity, and hundreds to her community, Catherine offered the "milk" of the "first principles of God's word"—fundamental spiritual doctrine. When she discerned that people had developed spiritually, she offered them the "solid food" of the mature (Heb 5:14).

In *Dear Parents*, she provided guidance to married couples and parents about how to live the Gospel in a secularized society, and how to raise children as disciples of Christ.[4] She emphasized the home as the heart of the world, observing that parents were preparing the future generations for that world.

In *Dearly Beloved: Letters to the Children of My Spirit*, she guided her own community with general spiritual teaching on how to live the Gospel without compromise, especially on how to form a community of love. She "daily fed her children, in all their needs, with the bread of Gospel wisdom," applying the Gospel to every concrete situation.[5] Catherine's uncompromising spirituality is expressed in these writings as she applied the Little Mandate to particular vocations and circumstances with their attendant responsibilities.

To whatever group she addressed, Catherine encouraged people to respond to their role in the sanctification of the temporal order. She especially called upon the laity to offer themselves as victims with Christ and to be truly a priestly people for the salvation of the world.

> It is not enough for the Fathers of the Council to clarify, under the inspiration of the Holy Ghost, this all-important question of the laity for our age. It is also vitally important that the laity respond to that clarification, to that call, to that renewed concept of their tremendous role in the Church, the Mystical Body of Christ of which they are such an integral part.
>
> For these clarifications are binding. They leave no excuse for the Catholic layman to remain an inert, half-asleep, inactive

---

3. Ibid., 15.

4. Doherty, *Dear Parents*, vii.

5. Editors, introduction to Doherty, *Dearly Beloved: 1956–1963*, v.

Christian. They place each Catholic face to face with a tremendous responsibility for the restoration, renewal, re-Christianization of the whole world.

If we are members of the Mystical Body of Christ, then it follows that we are part of the sacrifice. For if our Head deigned to offer Himself to us as food, then we too are part of the offering, the victim, a priestly people that offer the Sacrifice.[6]

I now offer give brief examples of how Catherine blessed these other states of life with her charism of spiritual mother—as a *staritsa*.

DEAR SISTER

It must be noted that at the time of Catherine's writing to Sisters (1953), most of them were engaged in the education of youth. She wanted them to be aware of the new movements among the laity and to enlist their support.

In some of her opening comments, Catherine prophetically anticipates the challenging and positive attitude of John Paul II towards youth. Are the Sisters bewildered, worried, discouraged about the attitude of young people today? This is *not* Catherine's experience:

Frankly, I am astonished at your finding this state of affairs. For I have ascertained that the contrary is true. Modern Catholic youth will journey thousands of miles to seek God and His truths. They will not hesitate to make immense sacrifices, financially and personally, to get to the places they think will give them the fullness of both. They just want that—*the fullness of God and His truths*. They are tired of sentimentality. They refuse to eat pap. They beg for the strong meat of the saints.[7]

Does this not remind us of the World Youth Days that were to come!

As a spiritual mother, Catherine tells the Sisters who they really are, and what they are capable of communicating to young people.

And you can do it. You, a woman passionately, completely in love with God, can teach others how to love your Love utterly. You, a saint in the making, can be a guide to their feet on the royal road to Christ. You, a creature in search of her Creator, can take youth along on that search. You, a pilgrim of the Absolute, can lead others on the same pilgrimage. You, a song, can fill the heart

6. Doherty, "Priesthood of the Laity: A Meditation."

7. Doherty, *Dear Sister*, 14.

of youth with music. You, a flame, can set other hearts on fire. You, the spouse of the Crucified, can, better than anyone else, make of youth "fools for Christ's sake." You, the garden of the Father, can nourish his "little flowers." You, the delight of the Holy Ghost, can make Him known to others. You, Mary's companions, can teach youth how to pray. You, Martha's helper, can show them how love serves.[8]

Other "words" of the spiritual mother to Sisters included such matters as their role in the restoration of the home, giving modern youth a healthy attitude towards sex and the marriage vocation, a reminder that they are forming the mothers of the future, that they must teach youth the primacy of faith and religion in life, and an admonition not to shrink from calling them to the religious and priestly life.

Teaching the youth a faith understanding of *vocation* is a frequent topic in the letters, especially the sublime nature of the *lay vocation* in the Church—and this before Vatican II:

Remember, the Church is the laity as well as the priests and bish-ops. The laity is also called to be apostles. The great tragedy of our times has its roots in the fact that, for a while, this wondrous and immense truth was forgotten. Under the duress and stress of the Reformation the laity was relegated to a secondary place and lost the vision of its apostolic vocation. It lost the knowledge that ordinary men and women were, in their fashion, a great part of the royal priesthood of Christ.[9]

There is also such a thing as the single vocation. The Sisters were challenged to change their own personal attitudes to be able to teach these vocations properly.

In addition, Catherine, so desirous of their growth in Christ, does not hesitate to have them examine *their own* life of poverty:

Today I want to talk about poverty. The holy poverty that, through one of your vows, is your constant companion. Beautiful and beyond compare is that vow, making you handmaidens to Lady Poverty, shaping you daily into the likeness of Him who was born in a dirty manger and died naked on a roughly hewn cross.

8. Doherty, *Dear Sister,* 15–16.

9. Ibid., 34–35.

But today you have become a sign of contradiction to many.
To others a sign of bewilderment. And to many others—I hate to
say this, but say it I must—you are a sign of scandal![10]

In essence, Catherine is mothering the Sisters with the same spiritual food she has been giving to the priests and is now giving to her own spiritual children in a new lay apostolate of the Church. She asks the Sisters to become aware of this movement of the Holy Spirit in these times and to teach modern youth about its potential. She concludes her book: "For believe me, Sister, *this is the age of the Lay Apostolate of Catholic Action. And your participation in it, by the proper formation of the youth under your care, will some day be your glory in heaven.*"[11]

DEAR SEMINARIAN

In the 1940s, seminarians were writing to Catherine seeking her advice and spiritual guidance. Catherine brought these requests to a bishop who "bade me to continue answering, to the best of my ability, each of you, and to leave the results of my answers to God."[12] In *Dear Seminarian*, Catherine addressed a wide range of topics germane to priestly and spiritual formation, as the sampling that follows illustrates.

Catherine emphasized that the priests of tomorrow should strive for personal holiness, and she invited them to employ the supernatural means at their disposal, especially a life centered on the Holy Eucharist. A holy priest will be able to give the people "God in His fullness and beauty. It is through *you* that all of these graces, this knowledge, this love of God, will flow into their hearts. It is *you* who will *offer the Mass*. It is through *you* that Christ will become the Bread and Wine of future saints."[13]

Catherine tried to prepare the seminarians for the future challenges of the priesthood by offering them a way to persevere with zeal in their vocation.

Now, at the threshold of your ordination, you are aflame with zeal.
The love of God consumes you. Your soul is hungry for God's Eternal Hills. Nothing is too hard for you. In Him, through Him, with

---

10. Ibid., 45.

11. Ibid., 80.

12. Doherty, *Dear Seminarian*, 13.

13. Ibid., 64.

Him, for Him you are ready not only to die but also to live in His service, which, at times, is harder.

But tomorrow will come. And with it the cold winds of everydayness, of loneliness, of monotony, of obstacles, of ingratitude, of misunderstandings, of ridicule, of hardship, of seeming failure and the need to begin always all over again. What then?

Are you ready for all these and more—much more which cannot be told, but must be lived—day by day, hour by hour, in the endless Via Crucis that is the path of all who fall in love with Him who walked it first, but especially of His chosen ones?

You will be ready if you remember that you must lead by *example*. And that to get strength to do so, you must be close, oh, ever so close, to your model, Christ.[14]

Drawing from her own experience of the spiritual life, Catherine first attempted to nurture in them a love for prayer and adoration before the Blessed Sacrament:

Prayer is your life. There you will find strength, faith, and fortitude not only to persevere, but to become indeed *an alter Christus*, which you were always meant to be.

Your house will always be next to your church. If your days are busy for Him, there is always the night to pray before His very face. One hour at least before the Blessed Sacrament in each twenty-four, in the great silence of God, will help you over all the obstacles we discussed above.

Prayer will make you a giant running on the way to God. Do not neglect it. Do not allow the best and holiest of works of mercy to become to you the heresy of good works, or to take you away from prayer.[15]

Inspired by the Little Mandate, Catherine issued the challenge of imitating the poverty of Christ and its value in the pastoral ministry. Poverty brings a deeper identification with Christ and with all others because all are poor before God.

Be not concerned either as to what you eat or how you sleep. In a word, be really poor in spirit and reality. Nothing impresses men more than the touchable likeness of other men to Christ! Especially do they expect it in their priests. No matter what history may whisper to the contrary, no matter what they may tell you to your

14. Ibid., 65.
15. Ibid., 66.

face, they hunger for a glimpse of the Man who had nowhere to lay His head—in you.

It helps them to carry their many burdens, to face their grinding poverty, to solve their frequently unsolvable economic problems. Be poor.[16]

In the above passage, Catherine reminded them of the "hunger" people have to see Christ in his priests, which reflected a deeper spiritual hunger for God in the midst of an ever-increasing secularization of culture and morals, especially among modern youth. In the next letter, Catherine's words echo the question of Peter in the Bread of Life discourses of John's Gospel, "Lord, to whom shall we go? You have the words of eternal life" (John 6:68). She was again teaching the seminarians that people would turn to them, as future priests and icons of Christ, as they did to Jesus to fill the spiritual void in their lives.

Dear Friend, I must now speak to you of hunger, the hunger that you will have to fill tomorrow when you become a priest in the order of Melchisedek. You must prepare yourself now for the spiritual bread line that will encompass, surround, and almost overwhelm you. I speak of hungry hearts and souls. They hunger with a great and holy hunger for the green hills of the Lord, but leaderless, they may, in our tragic modern desert of secularism, materialism, and atheism, mistake the lying mirage for the real thing.

This is what I hear from lay people: 'We *want to be saints*, because a saint is one who loves God as He should be loved. We want to love Him that way. We want to make others love Him too. We want to learn not only to keep away from mortal sin, but to practice the opposite virtues well, and fully. We want to be apostles of Christ! To *whom shall we go* for guidance?' Indeed, to *whom* shall they go, my friend?[17]

In *Dear Seminarian*, Catherine satisfied the seminarians' hunger, and attempted to form them into future spiritual fathers, to feed the holy hunger in souls.

In other letters, Catherine wrote from the perspective of a lay apostle and spiritual mother, sharing advice about what it means to be a priest and what laymen need from their priests. In one letter Catherine appealed to the seminarians to involve the laity in the life and mission of the Church

16. Ibid.
17. Ibid.

and to form the laity in the faith, so they might participate in the life and mission of the Church. "Now you want to know what is your part in making us (the laity) *integrated Catholics, Christocentric Catholics, Catholics whose whole life reflects the Faith, day in and day out.*"[18]

Telling the seminarians that this goal may be accomplished primarily in the parish, she counseled them to "first teach us the Commandments of God. Show us that *they are indeed the Commandments of Love;* that each word speaks to us of *that love which is God;* and that, in the final analysis, they are but signposts on the road of love, happiness, and peace—which is also the road to life everlasting."[19]

One sees here Catherine's uncompromising emphasis on love, which lies at the heart of the Gospel vision of the Little Mandate. "Explain to us clearly, in simple words, that though there are ten of them, they really add up to only two. Two simple direct statements, commands, that mean love again—*love of God and love of neighbor.* Tarry on these two awhile, until we know more about God, who loved us *unto death.*"[20]

In Catherine's spirituality, love for God has clear social implications, as the Little Mandate commands: "Take up My cross (their cross) and follow Me, going to the poor, being poor." Therefore, she exhorts the seminarians to focus on this dimension of the Gospel and to relate every sphere of the temporal order to their participation in the common priesthood of the faithful. Catherine's advice here reflects what the Second Vatican Council's *Decree on the Apostolate of Lay People* taught fifteen years later.[21]

> Go on from there and show us, too, that we must prove our love of Him by loving our neighbor. Then when these simple, but stupendous truths have become part of us, move on to the next point and show us *the social implications* of the commandments and the Gospel.
>
> Teach us to see rightly who our neighbor is, and what our duties toward him are—in politics, economics, the social scene, the labor fields, and management. Then open wide to us *the whole of the sublime Doctrine of the Mystical Body of Christ, and connect it with the Liturgy of the Church,* especially the Mass, bringing this

18. Ibid., 37.

19. Ibid., 38.

20. Ibid.

21. See Vatican Council II, *Decree on the Apostolate of Lay People,* especially nos. 6–8.

infinite and always renewed Sacrifice right into our daily lives, making it the center of them.[22]

Finally, Catherine encouraged the seminarians to challenge the laity by preaching the Gospel without compromise. There are echoes of the Little Mandate's word "be a light to your neighbor's feet" in her invitation to "become a lamp to our brothers' feet." By living the Gospel without compromise, one becomes an "integrated Catholic" and carries the light of faith into the lives of others.

> Give us the *fullness of the Gospel*. Water down nothing of its austere yet joyous message. Be not afraid to ask much of us. Nay, ask all of us. We are much more likely to answer your challenge if it is great, fiery, and full of the love of God and us, than if you just ask a little of us, and so somehow leave us discontented and humiliated because we have not been found worthy of more.
>
> What will you ask of us, my friend? Not to sin? To go to Mass on Sunday? Is that all? Are we to go to God just on this? If only you show us the way, we can bring Him sanctity, a positive, glorious, singing life, which, while we live it (by its very nature) become a lamp to our brothers' feet. What is it going to be? Surely Christ Crucified is worth more than the minimum?[23]

DEAR PARENTS

In the book *Dear Parents*, Catherine attempts to answer an important question: "How can followers of Jesus Christ, in whatever circumstances, nurture their children and be supported themselves in a society where human life is cheap, where personal ambitions and material possessions are valued above everything else, and where God is forgotten, rejected, or unknown?"[24]

Catherine's answers are drawn from her own experience as a wife and working mother; from her painful annulment of her marriage from an unfaithful husband; and from her deep faith and understanding of Christian marriage with her very loving second husband, Eddie Doherty.

In 1952, in response to a personal request from Pius XII that her apostolate "should help to restore the home to Christ," Catherine established

22. Doherty, *Dear Seminarian*, 38–39.
23. Ibid., 39–41.
24. Doherty, *Dear Parents*, vii.

a summer outreach program at Madonna House called Cana Colony.[25] Families come to Cana Colony for a one week retreat in a rural setting. *Dear Parents* is based on Catherine's personal talks and letters to them, in which she applied the Gospel to their particular circumstances. This outreach to families continues to this day in Combermere.

Marriage: A Vocation to Love

Catherine's starting point is the Mandate's insistence on "love, love, love, never counting the cost," a love that leads to oneness or *sobornost* among the couples and their children. "For you see, marriage is a *vocation*, a call of God to two people to become one, found a home, beget, bear and raise children; and, in this glorious and very hard vocation, to become saints themselves, and to do all that is in their power to make saints of their children."[26]

Catherine emphasizes that marriage requires, like all Christian vocations, an undivided heart. She then attacked the root of so many marital problems—the divided heart:

> The greatest enemy of any vocation is a divided heart. How many parents are wholeheartedly occupied with, and concerned about, fulfilling this vocation of theirs as it should be filled—by serving God through it? If they were so concerned, then problem children, problem youth, and marital problems would almost vanish and, as the parents grew in holiness—which is love—these problems would vanish indeed.
>
> What do I mean by a divided heart? I certainly do not mean adultery, or obvious physical neglect of any marital or home duty. No. I simply mean trying to compromise what cannot be compromised. For instance, trying to serve God and mammon at the same time by putting a premium on values that are secondary—values such as money, power, position, status in the community, or social obligations, real or imaginary.[27]

25. Ibid., 4.
26. Ibid., 2.
27. Ibid.

Forming a Christian Home

Having diagnosed the problem, Catherine then offered a word that would heal and restore Christian family life. She began by challenging parents to examine their own consciences:

> What is their attitude to God and to each other? Do they understand that theirs is the vocation to love—and to love so well that their children will learn love by just being their children and going into the school of their love? Do they comprehend that love is total surrender—surrender to one another, for the love of God and each other? Do they understand that love never uses the pronoun "I" and is neither selfish nor self-centered? On the answer to these questions depends so much. Who can truthfully say when they are entering marriage that they know these answers?[28]

Catherine reminded married couples that on their wedding day "the two become one. The man and the woman leave parents and home and cleave to one another, becoming one flesh. (Gen 2:24) This means surrender, a giving of oneself until, in truth, the two become one flesh. For those who understand this—and alas, how few they are—the veil of faith becomes gossamer thin, especially at Communion, when husband and wife become one in the heart of Christ. Love unites them in a *sobornost* with each other and with Christ in the Holy Eucharist. This unity enables the couple to form a Christian home:

> That is where this oneness is felt most by those who believe, and believing, see. Oneness of vocation, of love, of mind, heart, soul and body—a man and woman bound by the soft, unbreakable bonds of an awesome sacrament—form a home.
>
> What kind of home is it? It truly does not matter if it is a palace, a hovel, or anything in between. You see, a home is not a dwelling built by hands. Rather, it is built by love, by that unity, that oneness that makes out of a hovel a palace of joy and peace, because the tranquility of God's order reigns in the heart of it.[29]

Catherine held a highly optimistic estimation of Christian love as the foundation for a balanced and healthy family life. It was her unshakeable conviction that mature love heals and restores because it provides security.

28. Ibid., 4–5.
29. Ibid., 6.

Such a home and all that goes into its making results in mentally healthy parents and children. Here there will be no juvenile delinquency, no marital problems, nor child-parent problems, because all who live in such a home will find love, and hence, security. These two things alone—love and security—promote that emotional health we call maturity, when the calendar years and the emotional years blend.[30]

The remainder of Catherine's advice focused on concrete ways to restore the home to Christ. She spoke to them about the necessity of prayer, how to combat secular influences, and provided answers to specific questions.

For example, one parent asked: "What do you think of teenagers between the ages of fifteen and eighteen going steady? Do you think it should be allowed?"[31] Catherine's response was negative because "going steady" implied the selection of a marriage partner, and teenagers are not emotionally mature enough to assume that responsibility. Her own experience of marriage as a teenager shaped this view: "It is quite obvious to anyone with an ounce of common sense that fifteen is much too early to think of marriage. I was married for the first time at fifteen, and I know what I'm talking about."[32]

Catherine discerned the heart of parents' questions about "going steady." They were seeking advice about how to form their children in Christian morals during the adolescent years. She returned to the theme of restoring the home to Christ.

Here is where parental authority must be exercised to the full. They [parents] want to know how to teach the vital truths of life to their children and how to make children and youth understand the infinite beauty, holiness and divine purpose of sexuality. The only answer is to make your home what it should be—a novitiate for your children for the sublime vocation of future married life! The answer begins almost in the cradle. We must restore the home to Christ.[33]

30. Ibid.
31. Ibid., 54.
32. Ibid., 55.
33. Ibid.

The Duty of the Moment

The Little Mandate says, "Do little things exceedingly well for love of Me." Catherine taught parents that another way to help restore Christian family life was in fulfilling the "duty of the moment." By doing so, the "tranquility of God's order" is fostered because its foundational motivation is self-sacrificial love.

> The duty of the moment is what you should be doing at any given time in whatever place God has put you. If you have a little child, your duty of the moment may be to change a dirty diaper. So you do it. But you don't just change that diaper, you change it to the best of your ability, with great love for both God and that child. Do you do it like that? You can see Christ in that child.
>
> Or your duty of the moment may be to scrub your floors. Do you scrub your floors with great love for God? If you see to it that your house is well-swept, your food is on the table, and there is peace during the meal, then there is this slow order that is established, and the immense tranquility of God's order falls upon you and your family. Yes, there is order, because we keep thinking of others, things get clear in our hearts. Then we can forget ourselves.[34]

Catherine's emphasis on love in fulfilling the duty of the moment taught parents how to love Christ in and through ordinary human activity, which was tantamount to an invitation to Christ to make his dwelling in the home. The divine presence sanctifies family life, and promotes the tranquility of order Catherine insisted was necessary to restore the home to God.

> Remember also that when you do the duty of the moment, you do something for Christ. You make a home for him, in the place where your family dwells. You feed him when you feed your family. You wash his clothes when you do their laundry. You help him in a hundred ways as a parent.
>
> There is something each of us has to do, my friends. First I have to be an icon of Christ. Then the icon must step out of my heart and wash the feet of my brother, for Christ said, 'I have come to serve you.'"[35]

Finally, in *Dear Parents*, Catherine taught parents and children how to share in the mission of restoring a secularized world to Christ. "Now,

34. Ibid., 61.

35. Ibid., 65.

how do you show the face of Christ to a world that is secular, atheistic, indifferent, greedy, and selfish? By doing what he asks of you. And his voice is very simple. He says, 'Love God with your whole life, your whole heart. And love your neighbor as yourself' (Matt 22:38–39). Now, just do as he tells you, and live your life for everybody. The place to start is with the duty of the moment."[36]

DEARLY BELOVED: LETTERS TO THE CHILDREN OF MY SPIRIT

A three-volume collection contains published letters from Catherine to her spiritual children in which she gives practical guidance about living the Gospel without compromise in every situation. The community considers these letters as one of its great treasures because in them, Catherine applied the gospel to every conceivable aspect of daily life. Frequently these letters to the community emerged from Catherine's personal prayer and meditation in the chapel, in the *poustinia*, or during her nightly vigils. In prayer, she received a word and then shared it with her spiritual children. Previous chapters in the present book are replete with examples from these letters. However, we offer here one more example, which is universal in its application to any state of life.

Curiosity and Gossip

Catherine had been meditating on the word "curiosity," and in this letter she shares the fruit of that meditation.

"In chapel one night I was meditating upon the word *curiosity*, and wondering why people are so curious about so many things that do not concern them. What is that inner compulsion which makes people want to know the details of every event, especially those concerning people 'who matter'? Curiosity wants to tear with its sharp fingernails (not caring how deeply it wounds) the veil of personal, normal reticence which surrounds every individual."[37]

Having summarized this human problem, she spoke of how this "sin against charity and justice, and the dignity of the human person" can be

36. Ibid.

37. Doherty, *Dearly Beloved: 1974–1983*, 223–24.

eradicated from community life. Writing as a spiritual mother, Catherine echoes the words of St. Paul: "I became your father in Christ Jesus through the Gospel. I urge you, then, be imitators of me" (1 Cor 4:15–16). Catherine lived the life of the community, and taught the Gospel by her personal example.

Here she shares what she does when in the presence of someone who gossips out of idle curiosity:

> I have to listen, because I cannot stop other people from talking, though I try. However, if this is impossible, then I simply say nothing. This usually acts like a cold shower. Definitely I never show any *curiosity*. I listen with a bored face which at least stems the flow of the gossip. At the end of the story I usually try in some gentle, charitable way to minimize the entire affair. I try to say something good about the person, and gently to point out the evil of gossip.[38]

Catherine then applies the Gospel to the problem in a deeper way and teaches her children the meaning of "wholesome curiosity"—a curiosity driven by the desire for God and the primary goal of restoring the world to Christ. One notes in this letter Catherine's steadfast adherence to the Gospel message and her undivided attention to its demands.

> Wholesome curiosity is interested in God and the things of God. This means the natural world, its beauty, and the human institutions of the world which we are to restore. Above all, I would welcome your curiosity about how to become saints in doing the works of the Apostolate. Have curiosity about everything which leads to *caritas* and all the other virtues through which you are going to restore the world to Christ. *Here your curiosity should be unlimited.*[39]

When necessary, Catherine was firm about warning her children of spiritual dangers. In this passage, she warns and challenges them to reflect on the folly of futile and destructive behavior.

> To those to whom this applies I give a warning: your immortal soul is in danger if you indulge in idle curiosity, for it leads away from *God.*
>
> To such persons and to everyone I direct the following questions: What does it benefit your soul, your growth in sanctity, your

38. Ibid., 225.

39. Ibid., 226

development as a lay apostle, to know the intimate details concerning the lives of prominent people in your community? What *does* it really matter? Why *do* you want to probe into the lives of others?

This certainly does not bespeak that modesty of mind, the chief characteristic of which is to remain silent at the feet of God. I desire this sinful curiosity to cease, for it destroys the morale of a house as nothing else can. Let no one at Madonna House be guilty of it as so many seem to be.[40]

The Formation of a Spiritual Daughter

In addition to general spiritual guidance to the community, Catherine formed individuals who were in leadership positions in the apostolate. One of the more notable among them was Theresa Davis, a member of Madonna House and one of Catherine's spiritual daughters.

Theresa Davis was a product of a solid Catholic family, attended a Catholic college, and went to daily Mass. In the summer of 1955, she and her sister were vacationing in northern Ontario, and the nearest place to attend Sunday mass was Combermere. Sometime later, Theresa was drawn back to Madonna House by "the grace of the place" and was introduced to Catherine.[41]

Theresa described her first meeting with Catherine as a graced encounter that "*indeed* changed my life. She talked about God and love; about loving God back passionately; about living the Gospel without compromise by doing the duty of the moment; about living a life of simplicity; about doing the 'little things' of daily life out of love, to save the world."[42]

Theresa became a member of the Madonna House Apostolate and took her final promises in April 1963.[43] She describes Catherine's spiritual motherhood in this way: "B [our nickname for Catherine] *took me in tow*, and over the next 40 years I *ingested her love and her vision* of the apostolate. Through correspondence with me during my assignments at Madonna House posts in Canada, the U.S., and around the world, B *applied the Gospel* to every situation I presented to her. She *formed me in the spiritual life*,

---

40. Ibid., 226–27.
41. Davis, *To Follow Christ*, 1.
42. Ibid.
43. Ibid., 3.

trained me to direct others, and led me to depths within myself that I did not suspect existed" (emphasis added).[44] In her letters to Theresa, Catherine can be seen forming Theresa in the Gospel in concrete, everyday circumstances. Catherine's words to Theresa about courage are useful to anyone facing situations that require courage in any age.

Fear and Courage

In 1963, Theresa was assigned as the local director of Madonna House in East Pakistan, along with two other staff workers, Joanne and Nancy—who also received letters of formation from Catherine. More frequently, however, Catherine addressed herself to Theresa, who was their superior, forming the others through her.[45] In East Pakistan at that time, violence was an ever-present danger. In a letter on September 18, 1963, Catherine gave Theresa a teaching about fear and how it can be conquered.

First, she addresses the very real dangers Theresa and her staff must face—disease, mob violence, acts of terrorism, and war.[46] Catherine then begins to form Theresa in the virtue of courage:

> Courage is not the absence of fear; on the contrary, if you were not afraid, you could not be courageous. Courage lies in *overcoming* fear because of a motivation: for a soldier, love of country; for a mother, protecting her children; for a man, protecting his family, etc. As lay apostles, our motivation—God and faith in God—is the greatest of all. Our courage finds its source and life in God and arises out of deep faith in Him. Yes, little TD, this is the time for courage. You must be the strength, the assurance, the courage for the other two. Otherwise, if they are not fearful, they will become fearful; and if they are fearful, they will become more so. Share the burden of your fears with me, but show the little ones no trace of it.[47]

44. Ibid.
45. Ibid., 1–2.
46. Ibid., 9.
47. Ibid.

Poverty and Obedience

In a letter to one of the other staff workers in Pakistan, Catherine outlined some fundamental principles of her spirituality, applying them to their service of the poor in East Pakistan. Catherine's teaching is basic doctrine that can be applied to anyone regardless of his or her station in life: we are all poor before God because we are creatures, dependent on God for everything. This is our fundamental poverty before our Creator:

> Now the time has come to understand that poverty is not only a virtue to practice; it is also a state, a way of life. Poverty is the fruit of love of God and the key to humility, which is truth. And since truth is God, poverty is a short-cut to God. Now you have to really, deeply, fully realize that all you are, all you have, is from God! From this it follows that you have and are nothing.
>
> Once you accept this truth of your own poverty before God, the very marrow of your thoughts, your life, your love, your body—in a word your very being—you will become truly humble. Then you will walk in TRUTH—walk in, and with, God.
>
> Here, then, is your first gift to those you have come to serve. You can equal their poverty, physical though theirs may be, by acknowledging your general poverty as a creature, your total dependence upon God! The acceptance of this truth will make you truly free, free to love and serve these poor, tragic people. It will also make you free to love and serve God more passionately, more constantly.[48]

After describing this general poverty, common to all men, Catherine insisted that these spiritual children were still only "on the *threshold* of poverty's dwelling."[49] This general poverty leads to the "hallway of *obedience*. A hallway is a place where people leave or hand over their outer garment. The hallway you are stepping into now is the hallway of faith, a place where you leave your garments. You let yourself be *stripped* of your garments. There is a big difference between 'taking off' and 'being stripped.' You will let yourself be stripped of your garments so as to stand even more naked before God and man."[50]

This stripping is their way of imitating Christ who surrendered his own will and allowed himself to be stripped naked to obey the Father's will,

48. Ibid., 14.
49. Ibid.
50. Ibid.

to identify more fully with the human race, and to offer himself as a sacrifice for the world's salvation. One may hear in these words veiled references to the Little Mandate—they are to take up the cross of the poor, "being one with them, one with Me," by identification and imitation:

> Yes, you will be as naked as Christ before His crucifixion. For you will have to relinquish, first and foremost, *your own will,* and do that of *another. Completely!* For the more completely you do this, *the more completely will you truly IDENTIFY yourself with those poor that you are writing about. And what is more, by this very identification, unseen and maybe unnoticed by man in general, will you heal those very poor you have come to serve!* Yes, *obedience* will make you truly *poor.* For through it you will have surrendered that tremendous, magnificent incredible gift of God that each man possesses—*your free will!*[51]

By doing so, they help to heal the poor, as Christ did through his identification with the human race, offering to God a most acceptable oblation of self:

> Think of it! Giving back to God the one thing that makes you, in a manner of speaking, like Him. The one thing that is truly worth giving to God. And doing this, giving Him this gift, exclusively out of love for Him. Giving it freely, with the full consent of that very same *free, magnificent, tremendous, human will.* Giving it back to Him to also offer Him this gift, this love-offering, for all those poor. That is the most beautiful facet of the priceless diamond we call *poverty.* Understand well this parable-letter, child. The poverty of which I speak is an *inner state of soul.*[52]

This poverty requires a continual stripping of the "shreds" of self-will:

> For instance, one of these shreds may be a desire for comfort; yet this must be taken off immediately. Another shred will be attitudes you will notice forming in you. Each of these has to be examined carefully, prayerfully, and dealt with accordingly, lest they interfere with that total nakedness, that total surrender. Thus, your life will be a continual *inner stripping of yourself.* It will never end until you enter into His eternal kingdom.
>
> Perhaps now you understand better *that poverty leads to obedience; obedience, to total surrender; total surrender, to death to*

---

51. Ibid., 15.
52. Ibid.

self; death to self, to resurrection and growth in the Lord. All this beginning *HERE and NOW on this earth!*[53]

Catherine's teaching here on poverty, while specifically addressed to her spiritual children who were attempting to live the Madonna House vocation, is useful for anyone consecrated to God through obedience—religious, monastic communities, and diocesan priests. It offers a way to understand the spiritual meaning of obedience through the prism of poverty, which can perhaps lighten its burden and help appreciate its supernatural efficacy and value.

Chastity

Theresa wrote to Catherine in 1964 to express concerns about living chastely in the foreign missions. In the following letter, Catherine gave her prudent advice on how to practice this virtue. She suggested that her three spiritual children—being young, alone, and feminine—could become sources of temptation for other men. Because they were in a largely Muslim country, they would have to take extra precautions to guard this virtue.

> Especially in mission lands of the East, chastity of glance, of gesture, of walk, of speech—perfect chastity—is your virtue. You must conquer even gestures of our culture that in North America would never be considered unchaste, that in fact would be considered quite modest. This is the crucible, the cross of your adaptation for you.
>
> It behooves you as Local Director to be very watchful, but also to use all means, especially days of recollection, retreats, and days of *poustinia,* to hammer this virtue of chastity deeply into the consciousness of each of you, yourself included. Being human, you have to keep it before you all the time. Daily in your prayers you must ask for the grace. On the basis of this virtue is determined the effectiveness of your apostolate. Share these thoughts with the others.[54]

Theresa's response to Catherine reveals the positive fruit of Catherine's spiritual motherhood. Her spiritual children are maturing in "so many areas" as a result of her constant nurturing and guidance:

53. Ibid.

54. Ibid., 33–34.

I received your letter of February 24th and the staff letter discussing chastity. The three of us read these letters together. They were absolutely beautiful, positive, inspiring, and topical. The three of us are seeing the problem of chastity more deeply, and we realize more deeply our responsibility. Nothing but good has come from this whole situation and from your letters. My heart bursts with joy when I think of how we three are growing together and deeply in so many fields, in so many areas. If we return to Canada in a couple of months, this half year will have been more than worth it simply in terms of what we have already learned and how we have already matured.[55]

The Word of Staritsa Catherine

In the following letter, written on July 25, 1964, Catherine addresses herself to all three of her spiritual children. This letter is important, for it reveals Catherine's tenderness in mothering these young women so far from their native country. Sensing, as a good mother can, that her children are in a crisis, Catherine suggests that she would like to visit them personally; she desires to share in and take on their burdens; she consoles them by saying that she has offered herself and her prayers to God on their behalf. She has begged God for a "word" of grace for them:

> I think it is time that I should come for a visit. For I sense, even more than I know, that either all of you or some of you are passing through a crisis. So I want to come and *console you and give you strength and share with you in some of your confusion—in some of your bewilderment, in some of your hurts*—and tell you about the joy of the Lord that is hidden in every one of you.
>
> True, by myself I couldn't do this. Only Christ can do it. So I have beseeched Him for the last few weeks *constantly on your behalf! I prayed for you* at dawn. I have prayed for you at Mass. *I have offered my days for you, and my night prayers too.* For I love you much. And though I haven't been yet to Pakistan, *I am really there with you.* So I beg the Lord Christ humbly, reverently, and forcibly to *give me words—His words—to console you, strengthen you, and clarify for you things that trouble you* [emphasis added].[56]

55. Ibid., 34.
56. Ibid., 40.

In September, 1965, war erupted between India and China, with East Pakistan allied with China. Theresa wrote to Catherine, telling her that an evacuation of some missionaries had taken place, and that she and her staff had been "advised strongly to leave."[57] She asked for Catherine's prayers and reflected on what her time in East Pakistan had meant to her. Her experience of poverty had born fruit in love for the people of that region: "Because only through poverty can we really show our love, our identification, our oneness."[58]

Catherine spent three days fasting and praying in the *poustinia* for them, and then recalled them home to Canada until the war was over.[59] In fact, they never returned to East Pakistan, but Catherine's spiritual motherhood had born fruit in the Spirit: "The experience of those few years marked each of our souls, minds, and hearts indelibly. It is our hope that her words will touch the hearts of all who share in these letters with the fire of the Gospel."[60]

57. Ibid., 57.
58. Ibid., 58.
59. Ibid.
60. Ibid.

Appendix

Chronology
The Life of Catherine de Hueck Doherty

August 15, 1896—Catherine's birth in Nizhny-Novgorod to Theodore and Emma Kolyschkine.

1903—Catherine's family moved to Alexandria, Egypt, where her brother Serge was born, and where, in a Catholic school, she received her first formal education. During this time her family traveled back and forth between Egypt and Russia.

1906–1907—Catherine's family lived in Paris, France.

1908–1911—The family moved back to Russia and lived in St. Petersburg.

January 25, 1912—Catherine married Boris de Hueck in St. Petersburg.

1914—Boris served at the Russian front during World War I with the Imperial Royal Engineers.

1915–1918—Boris and Catherine both served at the Russian front. Catherine nursed wounded soldiers. At various times they were able to return to Petrograd, where, with the beginnings of the Bolshevik Revolution, they experienced terror and hunger. In late 1917, they fled to the family estate in Finland, where they were seized in their home by Finnish Bolsheviks who sentenced them to death by starvation. Here Catherine uttered the prayer that apparently saved her life: "If you save me from this, I will give my life to you." After weeks of tortuous starvation, they were rescued by White Finnish forces. From there they volunteered with the White Russian army and were stationed in Murmansk.

October, 1919 —Catherine and Boris left for Scotland, then went to England.

November, 1919—Catherine entered the Catholic Church in the diocese of Westminster.

March, 1921—Catherine and Boris sailed to Canada and settled in Toronto. Their son, George, was born in July.

1924—Catherine began to work as a lecturer, first in Canada and then in the United States.

1926—Catherine lectured for the Catholic Union upon the recommendation of the Most Reverend Neil McNeil, Archbishop of Toronto. The Catholic Union later became the Near East Catholic Welfare Association. She met Father Paul Wattson, SA.

1928—Catherine lectured for the Leigh-Emmerich Lecture Bureau and became their promotional manager. She traveled to Europe as its representative.

1930-1931—Catherine was in Montreal. During this period, she and Boris separated and began proceedings for an annulment.

1932—Catherine made a survey for Archbishop McNeil regarding the inroads of Communism among Catholics in the Toronto area.

1933-1934—Catherine lectured on Communism, social justice, and Catholic Action. After receiving the blessing of Archbishop McNeil, Catherine moved into the slums of Toronto and began organizing youth groups and a core of volunteers to begin working among the poor.

June 24, 1934—Initiation of the Guild of Our Lady of the Atonement and the reception of members.

October 15, 1934—The official opening of Friendship House, Toronto.

February, 1936—Catherine opened a Friendship House in Ottawa. Study clubs spread to Hamilton, Ontario and Montreal, and Catherine began a newspaper, "The Social Forum."

Summer, 1936—Rumors circulated concerning Catherine and Friendship House

September, 1936—The new Archbishop of Toronto, James McGuigan, appointed a committee to investigate Friendship House.

December, 1936—Friendship House Toronto closed.

1937—Catherine wrote articles and set sail for Europe as a correspondent for religious publications.

1938—Father Paul Wattson, SA, of Graymoor helps Catherine set up a new Friendship House in Harlem, New York. The Friendship House movement spread with houses in Chicago, Marathon, WI; Portland, OR; Shreveport, LA; Washington, DC; and Burnley, VA.

March 18, 1943—The Archdiocese of Montreal Marriage Tribunal issued a Decree of Nullity of Catherine's marriage to Boris.

June 25, 1943—Catherine married to Edward J. Doherty, a well-known Chicago journalist, by the Most Reverend Bernard Sheil, Auxiliary Bishop of Chicago.

1947—Boris died. Catherine and Eddie moved to Combermere, Ontario, and opened a rural apostolate, first known as Friendship House (Canadian Branch) and later as Madonna House Apostolate, which developed into an international Catholic community of laymen, laywomen, and priests. Presently there are about 200 members and 19 field houses throughout the world.

October 30, 1955—Catherine and Eddie took promises of poverty, chastity, and obedience.

1956—Catherine resigned from the Executive Board of Friendship House, USA.

August 15, 1969—At the age of 79, Eddie Doherty was ordained a priest of the Melkite Rite of the Catholic Church by Archbishop Joseph M. Raya.

May 4, 1975—Father Eddie Doherty died.

August 15, 1978—Madonna House Constitution approved by Bishop James R. Windle, and the full membership of Madonna House (priests, laymen and laywomen) was erected as a Pious Union.

December 14, 1985—Catherine fell asleep in the Lord in her cabin in Combermere.

Bibliography

Allen, Joseph J. *Inner Way: Toward a Rebirth of Eastern Christian Spiritual Direction.* Brookline, MA: Holy Cross Orthodox, 2000.

Briére, Father Emile. "Catherine and Father Eugene Cullinane." n.d. TMs (photocopy). Madonna House Archives, Combermere, Ontario.

———. *Katia: A Personal Vision of Catherine de Hueck Doherty.* Sherbrooke, QC: Paulines, 1988.

Burton-Christie, Douglas. *The Word in the Desert: Scripture and the Quest for Holiness in Early Christian Monasticism.* Oxford: Oxford University Press, 1993.

Callahan, Father John. "Confidential Notebook." n.d., TD (photocopy). Madonna House Archives, Combermere, Ontario.

Climacus, John. *The Ladder of Divine Ascent.* Translated by Colm Luibheid and Norman Russell. New York: Paulist, 1982.

Congregation for the Clergy. *The Priest, Pastor and Leader of the Parish Community.* 4 August 2002. Vatican City: Libreria Editrice Vaticana.

Corcoran, Donald, Sr. "Spiritual Guidance." In *Christian Spirituality I: Origins to the Twelfth Century*, edited by Bernard McGinn, John Meyendorff, and Jean Leclercq, 444–52. New York: Crossroad, 1989.

Cullinane, Father Eugene. "A Meditation Stimulated by Catherine's Talk to Madonna House Priests." March 31, 1974. TMs (photocopy). Madonna House Archives, Combermere, Ontario.

———. "Newsletter to the Madonna House Family." 1 August 1974. Madonna House Archives, Combermere, Ontario.

Davis, Theresa. *To Follow Christ: Letters of Catherine Doherty to A Daughter in the Spirit.* Combermere, ON: Madonna House, 1998.

De Fiores, Stefano, ed. *Jesus Living In Mary: Handbook of the Spirituality of St. Louis Marie de Montfort.* Bay Shore, NY: Montfort, 1994.

Dubay, Thomas, SM. *Seeking Spiritual Direction.* Ann Arbor, MI: Servant, 1993.

Doherty, Catherine de Hueck. *Beginning Again: Recovering Your Innocence and Joy through Confession.* Combermere, ON: Madonna House, 2004.

———. *Catherine de Hueck Doherty: Essential Writings—Modern Spiritual Masters.* Edited by David Maconi. Ossining, NY: Orbis, 2009.

———. *Correspondence with Father Henry Carr: 1935–1961.* TLS (photocopy). Madonna House Archives, Combermere via Archives of the Congregation of Saint Basil, Toronto.

———. *Correspondence with Father Paul Wattson, SA of Graymoor: 1935–1937.* TLS (photocopy). Madonna House Archives, Combermere, Ontario.

————. *Correspondence between Catherine Doherty and Father Eugene Cullinane: 1964–1980*. TLS (photocopy). Madonna House Archives, Combermere, Ontario.

————. *Correspondence between Catherine Doherty and Father Sean [pseudo.]: 1965–1970*. Madonna House Archives, Combermere, Ontario.

————. *Correspondence between Catherine de Hueck and Spiritual Directors*. TD Madonna House Archives, Combermere, Ontario.

————. *Correspondence with Father John Callahan: 1951–1955*. TLS (photocopy). Madonna House Archives, Combermere, Ontario.

————. "Crimson Red." *Journey Inward*. Vol. 2. 3 January 1953. TMs (photocopy). Madonna House Archives, Combermere, Ontario.

————. *Dear Father*. Edited by Father Patrick McNulty and Marian Heiberger. 3rd ed. Combermere, ON: Madonna House, 2001.

————. *Dear Parents: A Gift of Love for Families*. Combermere, ON: Madonna House, 1997.

————. *Dear Seminarian*. Combermere, ON: Madonna House, 1989.

————. *Dear Sister*. Milwaukee: Brice, 1953.

————. *Dearly Beloved: Letters to the Children of My Spirit*. Vol. 1, 1956–1963. Combermere, ON: Madonna House, 1988.

————. *Dearly Beloved: Letters to the Children of My Spirit*. Vol. 3, 1974–1983. Combermere, ON: Madonna House, 1990.

————. "I Crown You With a Crown of Thorns." January 4, 1953. TMs (photocopy). Madonna House Archives, Combermere, Ontario.

————. *In the Footprints of Loneliness*. Combermere, ON: Madonna House, 2003.

————. *Journey to the Heart of Christ: The Little Mandate of God to Catherine Doherty*. Edited by Robert Wild. 2nd ed. Combermere, ON: Madonna House, 2013.

————. *Light in the Darkness: A Christian Vision for Unstable Times*. Combermere, ON: Madonna House, 2008.

————. "The Little Mandate." April 27, 1968. TMs (photocopy). Madonna House Archives. Combermere, Ontario.

————. *Lubov: The Heart of the Beloved*. With illustrations by Donna Suprenant. Locust Valley: Living Flame, 1985.

————. "The Mandate of God to Catherine." May 16, 1966. TLS (photocopy). Madonna House Archives, Combermere, Ontario.

————. *Molchanie: The Silence of God*. Combermere, ON: Madonna House, 1991.

————. *Mystical Body of Christ: Family of God, the Church*. 1st ed. Combermere, ON: Madonna House, 2013.

————. *Nazareth Family Spirituality*. Compiled and edited by Fr. Blair Benard. Combermere, ON: Madonna House, 2013.

————. "Of This and That." *Restoration* (1951) 423.

————. *On the Cross of Rejection*. Combermere, ON: Madonna House, 2003.

————. "An Open Letter to Priests." n.d. TL (photocopy). Madonna House Archives, Combermere, Ontario.

————. *Private Vow of Poverty*. February 2, 1952. TDS (photocopy). Madonna House Archives, Combermere, Ontario.

————. *Private Vows of Poverty, Chastity and Obedience*. October 30, 1955. TDS (photocopy). Madonna House Archives, Combermere, Ontario.

————. *Poustinia: Christian Spirituality of the East for Western Man*. Combermere, ON: Madonna House, 1993.

————. "The Priesthood of the Laity." *Restoration* (1969) 7–8.

————. *Re-Entry into Faith*. Combermere, ON: Madonna House, 2012.

————. *Sobornost*. 2nd ed. Combermere, ON: Madonna House, 2000.

————. *Spiritual Diary*. December 3, 1953. TMs Madonna House Archives, Combermere, Ontario.

————. *The Stations of the Cross: In the Footsteps of the Passion*. 3rd. ed. Combermere, ON: Madonna House, 2004.

————. *Strannik: The Call to Pilgrimage for Western Man*. Combermere, ON: Madonna House, 1991.

————. "Talk to Madonna House Priests." March 28, 1974. TMs (photocopy). Madonna House Archives, Combermere, Ontario.

————. *Where Love Is, God Is*. Milwaukee: Bruce, 1953.

Duquin, Lorene Hanley. *They Called Her the Baroness*. Combermere, ON: Madonna House, 1995.

E., Brother [pseudo.]. *Letter to Catherine de Hueck, New York*. March 4, 1941. TLS, Madonna House Archives, Combermere, Ontario.

Father Sean, *Catherine Doherty Roundtable*. Combermere, ON: Madonna House Archives. June, 1999.

Forman, Sr. Mary. "Desert Ammas: Midwives of Wisdom." *Nova Doctrina Vetusque* 207 (1999) 187–201.

Furfey, Paul Hanly. *Correspondence between Paul Hanly Furfey and Catherine de Hueck Doherty: 1938–1979*. TLS, Paul Hanly Furfey Papers. Archives of the Catholic University of America, Washington, DC.

Garrigou-LaGrange, Reginald. *The Three Ages of the Interior Life*. 2 vols. Translated by Sister M. Timothea Doyle. Rockford: Tan,1989.

————. *Spiritual Direction in the Early Christian East*. Translated by Anthony P. Gythiel. Kalamazoo, MI: Cistercian, 1990.

Gould, Graham. "A Note on the *Apophthegmata Patrum*." *Journal of Theological Studies* 37 (1986) 133–38.

John XXIII. *Mater et Magistra* (Encyclical Letter on Christianity and Social Progress) 15 May 1961. AAS 53 (1961) 401–64. English translation: *Encyclical Letter of His Holiness Pope John XXIII on Christianity and Social Progress*. Washington, DC: National Catholic Welfare Conference, 1961.

John Paul II. *Vita Consecrata* (Post-Synodal Apostolic Exhortation, The Consecrated Life) 25 March 1996. AAS 88 (1996) 378–486. English translation: *Post-Synodal Apostolic Exhortation of the Holy Father John Paul II on the Consecrated Life*. Edited by Daughters of St. Paul. Boston: Pauline, 1996.

————. "Ecumenical Dialogue Must Be An Indispensable Priority." *L'Osservatore Romano* 26 (June 24, 2001) 1–12.

John Paul II. Pontificium Consilium Pro Laicis. "Address of His Holiness Pope John Paul II on the Occasion of the Meeting with the Ecclesial Movements and the New Communities," nos. 6–7. In *Movements in the Church: Proceedings of the World Congress of the Ecclesial Movements Rome, 27–29 May 1998*, 222–23. Vatican City: Pontificium Consilium Pro Laicis, 1999.

Kontzevich, I. M. *The Acquisition of the Holy Spirit in Ancient Russia*. Edited by the St. Herman of Alaska Brotherhood. Translated by Olga Koshansky. Platina, CA: St. Herman of Alaska Brotherhood, 1988.

Lonsdale, David. "Towards a Theology of Spiritual Direction." *The Way* 32 (1992) 312–19.

Bibliography

Louf, André. "Spiritual Fatherhood in the Literature of the Desert." In *Abba: Guides to Wholeness and Holiness East and West*, edited by John R. Sommerfeldt, 37–63. Kalamazoo, MI: Cistercian, 1982.

McCorkell, Edmund J. *Henry Carr—Revolutionary*. With a foreword by Claude T. Bissell. Toronto: Griffin House, 1969.

McGuigan, Archbishop James C. *Letter to Father Paul Wattson, SA, Graymoor*. August 15, 1936. Archives of the Roman Catholic Archdiocese of Toronto, Archbishop Neil McNeil fonds, MN AP02.108b, Catherine de Hueck Series.

Meehan, Brenda. *Holy Women of Russia*. San Francisco: HarperSanFrancisco, 1993.

Newman, Barbara. *Gods and Goddesses: Vision, Poetry, and Belief in the Middle Ages*. Philadelphia: University of Pennsylvania Press, 2003.

Palladius. *The Lausiac History*. Edited by Johannes Quasten, Walter J. Burghardt, and Thomas Comerford Lawler. Translated by Robert T. Meyer. Ancient Christian Writers 34. Westminster, MD: Newman, 1965.

Parente, Pascal P. *Spiritual Direction*. Rev. ed. New York: Society of St. Paul, 1961.

Peterson, Joan M., ed. and trans. *Handmaids of the Lord: Contemporary Descriptions of Feminine Asceticism in the First Six Christian Centuries*. Kalamazoo, MI: Cistercian, 1996.

Pourrat, Pierre. *Christian Spirituality*. Vol. 4, *From Jansenism to Modern Times*. Translated by Donald Attwater. Westminster, MD: Newman, 1955.

Royo-Marin, Antonio, and Jordan Aumann. *The Theology of Christian Perfection*. New York: Foundation for a Christian Civilization, 1987.

Soler, Josep M. "The Desert Mothers and Spiritual Maternity." *Theology Digest* 36, no. 1 (1989) 31–35.

Shook, Laurence K. "Sermon Preached at the Funeral Mass of the Reverend Henry Carr, C.S.B." December 2, 1963. St. Basil's Church, Toronto, TD Madonna House Archives, Combermere, 85–87.

Swan, Laura. *The Forgotten Desert Mothers*. Mahwah, NJ: Paulist, 2001.

Thaisia, Abbess of Leushino. *Letters to a Beginner: On Giving One's Life to God*. 2nd ed. Wildwood, CA: St. Xenia Skete, 1996.

Vatican Council II. *Apostolicam Actuositatem* (Decree on the Apostolate of Lay People) 18 November 1965. *AAS* 58 (1966) 837–64. English translation: In *The Conciliar and Post-Conciliar Documents of Vatican Council II*, edited by Austin Flannery, 766–98. Northport, NY: Costello, 1992.

———. *Lumen Gentium* (Dogmatic Constitution on the Church) 21 November 1964. *AAS* 57 (1965) 5–71. English translation: In *The Conciliar and Post-Conciliar Documents of Vatican Council II*, edited by Austin Flannery, 350–426. Northport, NY: Costello, 1992.

Ward, Benedicta. *The Sayings of the Desert Fathers: The Alphabetical Collection*. With a preface by Metropolitan Anthony. Kalamazoo, MI: Cistercian, 1975.

———. "Spiritual Direction in the Desert Fathers." *The Way* (1984) 61–69.

Wattson, Paul. *Letter to the Most Reverend Pascal Robinson, Dublin*. June 7, 1937. TLS, Madonna House Archives, Combermere, Ontario.

Wild, Robert. *Catherine: A Newsletter to Promote the Cause for Canonization of Catherine de Hueck Doherty* 4 (2002) 1–8. Combermere, ON: Madonna House.

———. *Journey to the Heart of Christ*. Combermere, ON: Madonna House, 1953.

Recommended Reading

Ange, Daniel. *L'étreinte de feu: L'icône de la Trinité de Roublov.* Paris: Le Sarment, 2000.

Angell, Charles, and Charles LaFontaine. *Prophet of Reunion: The Life of Paul of Graymoor.* New York: Seabury, 1975.

Anson, Peter. *The Call of the Desert: The Solitary Life in the Christian Church.* London: SPCK, 1964.

Arseniev, Nicholas. *Russian Piety.* Translated by Asheleigh Moorhouse. Crestwood, NY: St. Vladimir's Seminary Press, 1964.

Aumann, Jordan. *Christian Spirituality in the Catholic Tradition.* San Francisco: Ignatius, 1988.

Aumann, Jordan, Thomas Hopko, and Donald G. Bloesch. *Christian Spirituality East & West.* Chicago: Priory, 1968.

Bazzett, Mary. *The Life of Catherine de Hueck Doherty.* Combermere, ON: Madonna House, 1998.

————. *The Life of Eddie Doherty.* Combermere, ON: Madonna House, 1998.

Beck, Jeanne R. "Contrasting Approaches to Social Action: Henry Somerville, the Educator and Catherine de Hueck, the Activist." In *Catholics at the Gathering Place,* edited by Mark George McGowen and Brian P. Clarke, 213–32. Toronto: Canadian Catholic Historical Association, 1993.

Bouyer, Louis. *History of Christian Spirituality: The Spirituality of the New Testament and the Fathers.* Vol. 3, *Orthodox Spirituality and Protestant and Anglican Spirituality,* London: Burns and Oates, 1960.

Bulgakov, Sergius. *The Orthodox Church.* Translated by Lydia Kesich. Rev. ed. Crestwood, NY: St. Vladimir's Seminary Press, 1988.

Cassian, John. *The Conferences.* Translated by Boniface Ramsey. ACW 57. Mahwah, NJ: Paulist, 1997.

Catechism of the Catholic Church. New York: Catholic, 1994.

Cea, Emeterio de, ed. *Compendium of Spirituality.* Vol. 1. Translated by Jordan Aumann. Staten Island: Alba House, 1995.

Chariton, Igumen. *The Art of Prayer: An Orthodox Anthology.* Translated by E. Kadloubovsky and E. M. Palmer. London: Faber and Faber, 1966.

Code of Canon Law. Translated by Canon Law Society of America. Washington, DC: Canon Law Society of America, 1983.

Corneau, Metropolitan Nicolae. "The Jesus Prayer and Deification." *St. Vladimir's Theological Quarterly* 39 (1995) 3–24.

Recommended Reading

De Guibert, Joseph. *The Theology of the Spiritual Life*. Translated by Paul Barrett. New York: Sheed and Ward, 1953

Doherty, Catherine de Hueck. *Apostolic Farming*. 2nd ed. Combermere, ON: Madonna House Archives, 2001.

———. *Bogoroditza: She Who Gave Birth to God*. Combermere, ON: Madonna House, 1998.

———. *Catherine Doherty Talks to Families*. Audiocassette. Combermere, ON: Madonna House, 2001.

———. "Christ Is Risen!" *Restoration* (1967) 5–6.

———. *Christmas Tales: From the Hearth of Catherine Doherty*. Audiocassette. Combermere, ON: Madonna House, 2001.

———. *Dearly Beloved: Letters to the Children of My Spirit*. Vol. 2, *1964–1973*. Combermere, ON: Madonna House, 1990.

———. *Donkey Bells: Advent and Christmas*. Combermere, ON: Madonna House, 2000.

———. *Doubts, Loneliness, Rejection*. Combermere, ON: Madonna House, 1993.

———. *An Experience of God: Identification with Christ—A Road to the Mystical Life*. Edited by Emile Briére. Combermere, ON: Madonna House, 2002.

———. *Fragments of My Life*. 2nd ed. Combermere, ON: Madonna House, 1996.

———. *Giving Your Life to God*. Audiocassette. Combermere, ON: Madonna House, 2002.

———. *God in the Nitty-Gritty of Life*. Combermere, ON: Madonna House, 2002.

———. *The Gospel of a Poor Woman*. Combermere, ON: Madonna House, 1992.

———. *The Gospel without Compromise*. Combermere, ON: Madonna House, 1989.

———. *Grace in Every Season*. Combermere, ON: Madonna House, 2001.

———. *In the Furnace of Doubts: Meditations—When You've Lost Your Answers*. Combermere, ON: Madonna House, 2002.

———. "Journey Inward." *Restoration* (1962).

———. *Journey Inward: Interior Conversations 1960—the Present*. Staten Island: Alba House, 1984.

———. *Kiss of Christ: Experiencing the Healing of Jesus through Confession*. Combermere, ON: Madonna House, 2000.

———. *Living the Gospel without Compromise*. New ed. Combermere, ON: Madonna House, 2002.

———. *Love One Another: A Talk on Living the Gospel*. Audiocassette. Combermere, ON: Madonna House, 2001.

———. "The Long Journey." *Queen of All Hearts* (1951).

———. "Madonna House." *Queen of All Hearts* (1953).

———. *Moments of Grace: From the Writings of Catherine Doherty*. Combermere, ON: Madonna House, 2001.

———. *My Heart and I: Spiritual Reflections 1952–1959*. With a foreword by Jean Fox. Petersham, UK: St. Bede's, 1987.

———. *My Russian Yesterdays*. Combermere, ON: Madonna House, 1990.

———. *Not without Parables: Stories of Yesterday, Today and Eternity*. 2nd ed. Combermere, ON: Madonna House, 1989.

———. *O Jesus: Prayers From the Diaries of Catherine de Hueck Doherty*. With an introduction by Lorene Hanley Duquin. Combermere, ON: Madonna House, 1996.

———. *Our Lady of Combermere*, Ontario. Combermere, ON: Madonna House, 1999.

———. *Our Lady's Unknown Mysteries*. Combermere, ON: Madonna House, 1990.

————. *The People of the Towel and the Water*. Combermere, ON: Madonna House, 1991.

————. *Season of Mercy: Lent and Easter*. Combermere, ON: Madonna House, 1996.

————. *Soul of My Soul: Reflections from a Life of Prayer*. Notre Dame: Ave Maria, 1985.

————. *A Talk on Sobornost*. Combermere, ON: Madonna House. 31 mins. 2001. Videocassette.

————. *Unfinished Pilgrimage: God's Little Mandate*. Combermere, ON: Madonna House, 1995.

————. *Urodivoi*. Combermere, ON: Madonna House, 1993.

————. "You Will Cover the Earth." *Restoration*. 50th anniversary ed. (1997).

Doherty, Eddie. *A Cricket in My Heart*. San Antonio: Blue Army, 1990.

————. *Tumbleweed*. 2nd ed. Combermere, ON: Madonna House, 1988.

Dreitcer, Andrew. "New Testament Images for Spiritual Direction." *The Way Supplement* 91 (1998) 50–61.

Edwards, Tilden H. *Spiritual Friend: Reclaiming the Gift of Spiritual Direction*. New York: Paulist, 1980.

Evdokimov, Paul. *The Struggle with God*. Translated by Sr. Gertrude. Glen Rock, NJ: Paulist, 1966.

Fedotov, G. P., ed. *A Treasury of Russian Spirituality*. New York: Sheed & Ward, 1948.

Flemming, David L., ed. *The Christian Ministry of Spiritual Direction*. St. Louis: Review for Religious, 1988.

Fox, Jean. *Inflamed By Love: Meditations for Spiritual Pilgrims*. Combermere, ON: Madonna House, 2002.

Goehring, James E. *Ascetics, Society, and the Desert: Studies in Early Egyptian Monasticism*. Harrisburg, PA: Trinity, 1999.

Gratton, Carolyn. *Guidelines for Spiritual Direction: Studies in Formative Spirituality*. Vol. 3. Edited by Adrian Von Kaam and Susan Annette Muto. Denville, NJ: Dimension, 1980.

Hausherr, Irénée. *The Name of Jesus*. Translated by Charles Cummings. Kalamazoo, MI: Cistercian, 1978.

Heiberger, Marian. *The Life of Father John Callahan*. Combermere, ON: Madonna House, 1999.

Iswolsky, Helen. *Soul of Russia*. New York: Sheed and Ward, 1943.

Jamart, François. *Complete Spiritual Doctrine of St. Therese of Lisieux*. Translated by Walter Van De Putte. Staten Island: Alba House, 1961.

John of the Cross, Saint. *Ascent of Mount Carmel*. Book II. Vol. 4 of *The Collected Works of St. John of the Cross*. With an introduction by Kieran Kavanaugh. Translated by Kieran Kavanaugh, and Otilio Rodriguez. Washington, DC: Institute of Carmelite Studies, 1979.

John Paul II. *Dominum et Vivificantem* (Encyclical Letter on The Holy Spirit in the Life of the Church). 18 May 1986. *AAS* 78 (1986) 809–900. English translation: *Encyclical Letter of John Paul II: The Holy Spirit in the Life of the Church and the World*. Edited by Daughters of St. Paul. Boston: Pauline, 1986.

————. "Message for the World Congress of Ecclesial Movements and New Communities." *L'Osservatore Romano* (June 10, 1998) 1–3.

————. *Pastores Dabo Vobis* (Post-Synodal Apostolic Exhortation, I Will Give You Shepherds). March 25, 1992. *AAS* 84 (1992) 657–804. English translation: *Post-Synodal Apostolic Exhortation of I Will Give You Shepherds*. Edited by Daughters of St. Paul. Boston: St. Paul, 1992.

Kadloubovsky, E. and H. E. H. Palmer, trans. *Writings from the Philokalia on the Prayer of the Heart.* 9th ed. London: Faber and Faber, 1977.

Leech, Kenneth. *Soul Friend.* London: Sheldon, 1977.

Lemieux, Dennis. *The Air We Breathe: The Mariology of Catherine Doherty.* New Bedford, MA: Academy of the Immaculate, 2010.

Lewis, Echo. *Victorious Exile: The Unexpected Destiny of Katya Kolyschkine.* Combermere, ON: Madonna House, 2013.

Manual of Eastern Orthodox Prayers. 2nd ed. Crestwood, NY: St. Vladimir's Seminary Press, 1983.

McPhee, Rosalie. *Marriage: Moments of Grace.* Combermere, ON: Madonna House, 2001.

A Monk of the Eastern Church. *Orthodox Spirituality: An Outline of the Orthodox Ascetical and Mystical Tradition.* 2nd ed. Crestwood, NY: St. Vladimir's Seminary Press, 1996.

Neyt, François. "The Prayer of Jesus." *Sobornost* 9 (1974) 641–54.

Palmer, G. E. and others, trans. *The Philokalia: The Complete Text.* Vol. 1. Boston: Faber and Faber, 1985.

Peters, Edward N., *The 1917 Pio-Benedictine Code of Canon Law.* San Francisco: Ignatius, 2001.

Pontificium Consilium Pro Laicis. *Movements in the Church: Proceedings of the World Congress of the Ecclesial Movements Rome, 27–29 May 1998.* Vatican City: Pontificium Consilium Pro Laicis, 1999.

Raya, Joseph Archbishop. *Byzantine Church and Culture.* Allendale, NJ: Alleluia, 1992.

———. *Theophany and the Sacraments of Initiation.* Combermere, ON: Madonna House, 1993.

———. *Theotokos: Mary, Mother of Our Lord God and Saviour Jesus Christ.* Combermere, ON: Madonna House, 1995.

———. *Transfiguration.* Combermere, ON: Madonna House, 1992.

Raya, Joseph Archbishop, et al. *The Divine and Holy Liturgy of St. John Chrysostom.* Allendale, NJ: Alleluia, 2001.

Ruffing, Janet. *Uncovering Stories of Faith: Spiritual Direction and Narrative.* New York: Paulist, 1989.

Ryan, Bill. "Inward Journey: The Spirituality of Catherine Doherty." *Canadian Review* 5, no. 8 (1987) 284–90.

Skobtsova, Mother Maria. *Mother Maria Skobtsova: Essential Writings.* Translated by Richard Pevear and Larissa Volokhonsky. Maryknoll, NY: Orbis, 2003.

Solovyev, Vladimir. *Russia and the Universal Church.* Translated by Herbert Rees. London: Bless, 1948.

Spidlik, Tomas. *The Spirituality of the Christian East.* Vol. 79. Translated by Anthony P. Gythiel. Kalamazoo, MI: Cistercian, 1986.

Tanghe, Omer. *As I Have Loved You: Catherine Doherty and Her Spiritual Family.* With an introduction by Archbishop Joseph Raya and Father Emile Briére. Translated by Omer Tanghe and Robert Wild. Dublin: Veritas, 1988.

———. *For the Least of My Brothers: The Spirituality of Mother Teresa and Catherine Doherty.* Translated by Jean McDonald. Staten Island: Alba House, 1989.

Thaisia, Abbess of Leushino. *The Autobiography of a Spiritual Daughter of St. John of Kronstadt.* Platina: St. Herman of Alaska Brotherhood, 1989.

Vatican Council II. *Ad Gentes Divinitus* (Decree on the Church's Missionary Activity). 7 December 1965. *AAS* 58 (1966) 947–90. English translation: In *The Conciliar and*

Post-Conciliar Documents of Vatican Council II, edited by Austin Flannery, 813–56. Northport, NY: Costello, 1992.

———. *Gaudium et Spes (Pastoral Constitution on the Church in the Modern World)*. December 7, 1965. *AAS* 58 (1966) 1025–120. English translation: In *The Conciliar and Post-Conciliar Documents of Vatican Council II*, edited by Austin Flannery, 903–1001. Northport, NY: Costello, 1992.

———. *Presbyterorum Ordinis* (Decree on the Ministry and Life of Priests). December 7, 1965 *AAS* 58 (1966) 991–1024. English translation: In *The Conciliar and Post-Conciliar Documents of Vatican Council II*, edited by Austin Flannery, 863–902. Northport, NY: Costello, 1992.

———. *Unitatis Redintegratio* (Decree on Ecumenism). November 21, 1964. *AAS* 57 (1965) 90–107. English translation: In *The Conciliar and Post-Conciliar Documents of Vatican Council II*, edited by Austin Flannery, 452–73. Northport, NY: Costello, 1992.

Ward, Benedicta. *Harlots of the Desert: A Study of Repentance in Early Monastic Sources*. Kalamazoo, MI: Cistercian, 1987.

———. *The Lives of the Desert Fathers*. With an introduction by Benedicta Ward. Translated by Norman Russell. Kalamazoo, MI: Cistercian, 1980.

———. *The Wisdom of the Desert Fathers*. Fairacres: SLG, 1977.

Wild, Robert. "Catherine Doherty and Vladimir Soloviev." *Eastern Church Journal* 1, no. 3 (1994) 59–77.

———. *Catherine's Friends: The Foundress of Madonna House and Her Friendships*. Ottawa, ON: Justin, 2011.

———. *The Chambers of Her Heart: Madonna House and Priestly Formation*. Combermere, ON: Madonna House, 1998.

———. *Journey to the Lonely Christ: The Little Mandate of Catherine de Hueck Doherty*. Staten Island: Alba House, 1987.

———. *Love, Love, Love*. Staten Island: Alba House, 1989

———. *Journey in the Risen Christ*. Staten Island: Alba House, 1992.

———. *Madonna House as a Divine Milieu: An Introduction for Visiting Guests*. Combermere, ON: Madonna House, 2015.

Wild, Robert, ed. *Compassionate Fire: The Letters of Thomas Merton and Catherine de Hueck Doherty*. Notre Dame, IN: Ave Maria, 2009.

———. *Comrades Stumbling Along: The Friendship of Catherine de Hueck Doherty and Dorothy Day as Revealed through Their Letters*. Staten Island: Alba House, 2009.

Wild, Robert, et al. *Living Fully in Our Time: Retreat Talks*. Combermere, ON: Madonna House, 2000.

Zernov, Nicholas. *St. Sergius: Builder of Russia*. Translated by Adeline Delafeld. London: SPCK, 1941.

———. *Three Russian Prophets*. London: SCM, 1944.